Real Estate Wholesaling for the Average Joe

Learn How to Invest in Real Estate even on a Low Budget

By Trevis White

The following Book is reproduced below with the goal of providing information that is as accurate and reliable as possible. Regardless, purchasing this Book can be seen as consent to the fact that both the publisher and the author of this book are in no way experts on the topics discussed within and that any recommendations or suggestions that are made herein are for entertainment purposes only. Professionals should be consulted as needed prior to undertaking any of the action endorsed herein.

This declaration is deemed fair and valid by both the American Bar Association and the Committee of Publishers Association and is legally binding throughout the United States.

Furthermore, the transmission, duplication, or reproduction of any of the following work including specific information will be considered an illegal act irrespective of if it is done electronically or in print. This extends to creating a secondary or tertiary copy of the work or a recorded copy and is only allowed with express written consent from the Publisher. All additional rights reserved.

The information in the following pages is broadly

considered to be a truthful and accurate account of facts and as such any inattention, use or misuse of the information in question by the reader will render any resulting actions solely under their purview. There are no scenarios in which the publisher or the original author of this work can be in any fashion deemed liable for any hardship or damages that may befall them after undertaking information described herein.

Additionally, the information in the following pages is intended only for informational purposes and should thus be thought of as universal. As befitting its nature, it is presented without assurance regarding its prolonged validity or interim quality. Trademarks that are mentioned are done without written consent and can in no way be considered an endorsement from the trademark holder.

Table of Contents

Introduction

Congratulations on purchasing this book and thank you for doing so.

The following chapters will discuss what real estate investing is and how you can get the most out of your money by letting it work for you. When it comes to making a real estate investment, there are a lot of things to consider and this book wants to get into details about every aspect needed to take conscious and smart investing decisions.

This book will provide you with valuable lessons, given by the best investors in the real estate market.
The goal of the book is to speed up your education and save you time and money along the way.

Before getting started, it is important to note something about mindset. This, as the other books in the series, do not offer "get rich quick solutions", since they do not exist. Especially when you are beginning your journey in investing, it is fundamental to focus on learning and acquiring new information, rather than just chasing money. With the right knowledge, results will come much faster and you will be amazed by what you can accomplish, even with minimal capital. The book wants to give you the tools you need to get started and share with you some of the golden nuggets that made other people wealthy. If you study this material carefully and start applying it, you will lay out the foundation for prosperity and wealth.

There are plenty of books on this subject on the market, thanks again for choosing this one! Every effort was made to ensure it is full of as much useful information as possible, please enjoy!

Chapter 1

What real estate investing is and a note about mindset

The activity of a real estate investor is often misunderstood. Most people, when hearing the term "real estate investor" think "ok, who does this job earns a lot of money, it is fun, it is easy to do and it is all sunshine and rainbows", but the reality is not like that. At all. This information that is disseminated all around the internet is not correct. The activity carried out by a real estate investor is a methodical activity, it is an activity that takes a long time to master. The investor has to visit lots of properties, he has to make a lot of proposals knowing that most of these offers will be rejected, as you can imagine.

It is important to operate with a large number of real estate visits and proposals to obtain results. In other words, the idea that the real estate investor walks and makes money is absolutely false; it is a very difficult job.

What I would like to tell you is that this is an extraordinary profession, where you can obtain very important personal and economic satisfactions, but it is necessary to work hard. It is necessary to have a lot of time and it is necessary to know from the beginning that it will not be easy. If you could automatically earn, everybody would do it, which is absolutely not real, we know it very well. To do something and get a result you need to commit, so if you are interested in the world of real estate investments you must know that it is a difficult job like all other investments. It is a job where you'll have to spend time, where most of the answers you receive will be no, you will not have to give up, you'll have to continue and if you manage to be consistent and do things the right way you will be able to clearly get results not only at the economic level but also at the level of personal satisfaction.

Before getting started with the 15 Golden lessons of real estate investing, it is important to make a quick note about mindset.

Your dream house is not an investment, did you know that?

The property owned, or the house of our dreams - or villa depends on the possibilities of each of us, has always been considered a sacred "asset" in America. A goal to be achieved as soon as possible at the cost of any sacrifice. And indeed we are the people with the highest percentage of homeowners. About 80% of Americans own a home. It does not matter if we take out mortgages for thirty years (sometimes even longer) with monstrous instalments that most often absorb around 50% of the income of an average family. The important thing is to "own" our home. Good, this is what smart people do, right?. False. Almost nobody that is rich lives in a place he owns. As Grant Cardone says "rent where you live and own what you can rent".

The question I want to ask you now is this: do you think buying a house is equivalent to buying an asset or a liability? The answer is clear and not debatable. Among the mortgage payment, various charges, government, and municipal taxes, when buying a house you buy a liability.

But we better explain the concept of liability. By liability, we mean everything that generates cash outflow from our family income statement. By contrast, by asset, we mean everything that generates positive cash flow. Example, I buy an obligation that usually brings a coupon, this coupon represents an income and therefore the obligation is an asset.

The sad truth of the American real estate market

But how strange: we make so many sacrifices to buy a house, yet we buy a liability? Yes, dear readers, in America, unfortunately, the investment property is almost completely unknown. In fact, there is no real estate market in the true sense of the word. And for the real estate market I mean the sale of an asset, in this case, the house, in order to realize a capital gain and therefore an investment income. Trades usually in America in the vast majority of cases are made because a couple decides to get married and then buy a house, or move after the coming of children, etc. In summary, following a family necessity and not for making an investment, as usually happens for financial or business investments

The ventures of real estate investing

But at this point, the question to be asked is this: is it possible to transform the purchase of a house from a liability into an asset and consequently obtain a monthly income or make a capital gain? Well, dear readers, the answer is fortunately yes! Not only is it possible, but it is desirable that each of us in the investment process of their assets dedicate part of the capital to real estate investments.

Real estate investing has some notable advantages, for example, it is possible to receive monthly income (rents) and at the same time realize capital gains at the time of sale. Not only. Precisely because of the characteristics of the market in consideration, such as the American one, the investment in real estate, in fact, is a more than secure investment, as the "home" good in America will hardly lose value.

The recent crisis has confirmed this theory. Practically in the whole world, the real estate market has undergone very heavy devaluations even in the order of 50-60%, not only in America but also in Spain, England, etc. In America, in fact, there was only a stagnation of prices and a lengthening of the time of purchase. But in fact, the market has not fallen below 5% (obviously should be made distinctions according to regions, city type of properties, central or peripheral, etc ...)

Chapter 2

5 Beginners lessons about real estate investing

1. Invest in houses that you will rent

We hypothesize to buy a house of $ 200,000 with a minimum investment of $ 40,000 (but there are banks that also finance 100% of the amount) and that with the rent we cover only the mortgage payment. Well, after 10 years assuming an average revaluation of 4%, our house has been revalued for a value of $ 296,000 c. a Which means that $ 40,000 has become 96,000 in 10 years. In practice, an annual profit of 14%. Not bad, I would say if compared to the yields of bonds and some liquidity/money funds that fill the wallets of Italian savers.

In reality, the above calculations are not complete. As they do not consider the purchase and sale charges (taxes, notary, etc ...) and the additional capital gain. In fact, paying the instalment of the silent, the tenant also pays us a portion of the capital loaned by the bank; which means that when we sell, in addition to the revaluation of $ 96,000, we will have to add the missing principal amount to be returned to the bank net of transaction costs.

2. **From liability to an asset**

We hypothesize that we managed to buy a good deal and that therefore the property, net of the mortgage and the charges, generates a small monthly income deriving from the rent. Suddenly what was a liability becomes a monthly income, even if only a few hundred dollars, it is an addition to your income.

3. **Buy only amazing deals, especially at the beginning**

In order for the rent to exceed the instalment of the silent, it is necessary to buy well. Buying a good deal means essentially at a good price. Opportunities are there, they simply have to be found. Some small suggestions:

- Avoid the agencies;
- Find private vendors;
- Walk around the neighbourhoods that interest you looking for property for sale;
- Talk to the doorkeepers;
- Attend the Auctions in court. Only this aspect should be explored with an ad hoc article. For the moment, it is enough to know that the system has become absolutely transparent and secure. So you just have to find the right opportunity. You can buy houses even with 30/40% discount on the real value;
- Read the announcements and identify the "needy" people to sell;
- Buy in central and/or valuable areas. It is the only guarantee for not having bad surprise;

4. **Apply leverage on your money**

Fundamental. We have seen that buying a house with an initial investment could even generate a monthly income. Well, let's imagine to replicate the investment with the same characteristics at least 3 times and we hypothesize to be able to get 300 / month from each of our rents (net of charges and taxes). In fact, with $ 900 / month of capital gain we are able to safely pay a good instalment of a mortgage for the purchase of another house, and here comes the nice, paid entirely with the revenue from the rents. I leave to you the imagination of how many times it is possible to replicate the above investment scheme and calculate the benefits. It is just amazing.

5. **Only take mortgages with fix interest rates**

When you engage in real estate investing, you are already taking a "business" risk; you do not need to take other risks, such as interest rate related risk. Let me explain better when buying an investment property I need to know exactly how much is the monthly exit (instalment + charges) in order to correctly calculate the expected cash flow. Only careful planning of income and expenses can lead to a correct real estate investment. The accuracy of the calculations can make the difference between a successful and a non-profitable investment.

Chapter 3

Is it still profitable to invest in real estate?

In this chapter, we talk about houses, rents and real estate, with the aim of finally debunking the myth linked to real estate investment.

Also because, unlike what you hear around, there are still some situations where you can invest in real estate and bring home a good performance, but this is only true in some special cases and above all under certain conditions.

What I can guarantee is that it is not a simple and trivial activity, as those who do not have experience, skills or simply want to take advantage of it want to make you believe.

On this topic I think that one of the most repeated

phrases in absolute is:

"Brick is an excellent investment. It is safe and never betrays. The value of the property always grows over time ".

But as you probably noticed, you are not exactly like that, as the price of houses has fallen considerably over the last few years.
We must, therefore, try to overcome popular beliefs and give an adequate answer to the question of the questions, namely:

Is it still worthwhile investing in properties today?

And to solve this doubt we can not rely on "hearsay" or "bar opinions", but we must rather rely on a serious and documented analysis of how things really are.
Every time I talk to someone with money, in 99% of cases we end up talking about real estate.

"That one is so rich that he owns the whole city"

"That guy collects an avalanche of money every month through his properties"

These and other similar discourses are generally used to indicate the wealth of people who, in the popular imagination, have built a fortune thanks to the brick.

To this is added the literature Made in USA that, if you are minimally interested in business, economic growth or finance, you inevitably have to read also, like the various Kiyosaki & co., Just to name a few, who have built their notoriety about the leitmotif "buy real estate and enrich yourself".

Investing in real estate: a safe investment after all?

If you talk about buying a big car, many may wonder if you actually can afford to keep it.

If you go on vacation with a certain frequency, someone mumbles that you are a spendthrift.

Even worse if you rely on an independent financial advisor or if you open a trading account to make investments.

They immediately label you as crazy!

However, if you declare that you have bought a $ 250,000 apartment to go and live or if you have purchased a property that is falling apart in the suburbs of the world, compliments are in abundance and nobody doubts the goodness of your choice.

This is because we are used to thinking that real estate investment is as safe as a government bond.

"The grandfather has paid the house 2 million, today is worth 200,000 dollars" (inflation, for heaven's sake, let's not go down that route please!).

Here is just one of the many data that you can check yourself on the progress of our "safe investment" from 2007 to 2016. The value of real estate has literally plummeted over a single decade (-28% in the best case).

Probably we are touching the fund and then go back, but the fact remains that those who bought in the pre-economic crisis, ie in the collective euphoria of the race to the brick, today saw the value of its investment strongly depreciated.

Who has had the need to get rid of their purchase has literally sold off or has remained with the weight on the rump for years, given the absence of a flourishing market ready to win the apartment.

The old reasoning on the security of real estate purchase collides with the harsh reality of the world that has changed significantly.
If your relatives bought in the post-war period, when there was a company to be rebuilt from scratch and so many cities practically did not exist, it is quite obvious to say that there has been a re-evaluation.

First, there were the stones, 30 years later there were cities. Until the 70s the population was young and procreated at great rates. From the 1990s onwards, population growth, in line with other Western countries, has been miserably arrested, only to reverse the trend.

We are always the same, we are older and there are no more avalanches of people and families willing to move, change cities and enrich the demand for apartments.

According to The American Institute of Public Opinions, today 80% of Americans live in a house owned, that is, the same Italians who are old and therefore do not move, do not have children and, all in all, can always stay in the first apartment in which they entered. In a nutshell, anyone who could buy a house has already done it.

All others either are not owners by choice or simply can not afford it and must live in rent.

The legislation on leases, among other things, is very unbalanced in favour of the tenants and getting a bad guy, in a historical era of changes and difficulties in employment, has become more frequent than anything else.

All this leads to a dutiful reflection.

If almost everyone has a home in which to live, if we are on average less young and less likely to travel, if we have now almost all poured near large urban centres leaving the suburbs, how can we think of a growth propulsive real estate market in the coming decades?

Well, now that I slapped you and I made you understand why the adage "the brick is a safe investment" is a commonplace of the past, we can try to understand when it becomes convenient by doing two calculations together.

Also because the fact that it is not so sure does not mean that there are no opportunities to be seized.

Investing in real estate: opportunities are there and will always be there
I wanted to warn you before entering the heart of the discussion.
After brainstorming of negative things, we come to the opportunities that the sector offers at this time.

First point: prices are at historic lows.

The collapse of prices can be a pain for those who sell, but an opportunity for those who buy.

Every market has its own precise movements and lives of ups and downs and even the real estate is not immune to all this. Specifically, in the real estate market, there are many people who, unfortunately, must sell because they have immediate liquidity needs.

If we add this aspect to the already huge amount of property in circulation, this means that, as there is so much offer, you can buy at relatively low prices compared to the past.

From this point of view, many innovations are spreading also in America.

Short term rentals are on the rise thanks to the explosion of portals such as Airbnb and Home Away. Thanks to the diffusion of cheap means of transport, people who go on holiday have increased considerably and do not disdain to stay in apartments rather than in hotels. Tourism in our country, overall, is in excellent health. According to the MIBACT statistical office, last year we exceeded the threshold of 50 million visitors and recorded an increase of about 5 million visitors compared to 2016.

Although our universities are not among the best in the world, they attract students from all over the country. From the outskirts to the cities, from the South to the North, every year many off-site students move to get their degree. In short, the question is there, but obviously, it is necessary to act selectively going to grasp the potential that only some areas, and not all without distinction, can offer.

Let me explain to you better what I mean by this statement.

The main tourist resorts will never go into crisis and the short rental market is quite benevolent with the owner because he does not have the familiar difficulties.
Large cities attract tourists, students, and workers who generally offer greater guarantees and with whom it is possible to sign contracts with shorter duration and, therefore, less exposed to the risks of residential rent.

Above all the centres of big cities are often the object of a specular development with respect to the suburbs, which become impoverished and depopulated.

People, especially wealthy people, prefer services to

the isolation of remote areas.

In short, investing in real estate is still possible, if you know how to do it!

Investing in real estate: let's do the maths!
Enough words, let's move on to the numbers.

I want to share with you the analysis I did in the summer of 2017, thinking about New York.
My hypothesis is based on the purchase of a property located in a strategic area because it is very close to the main university.

The idea of exploiting the investment is based on renting out-of-town students who come to the city to study.
The area I am talking about is well served by public transport and is quite lively from a commercial point of view. The district is largely inhabited by families, the elderly, workers or students. The rental market can be said to be good enough for the reason that ruled my choice.

Speaking of numbers, the price per square meter varies from $ 1,000 for properties to be completely renovated, up to $ 1,800 for apartments in good condition and ready to be inhabited. Wanting for a moment to estimate to be good negotiators, we can concretely think of bringing home a two-bedroom apartment to renovate with $ 50,000. Obviously, we are also building experts and we select an apartment that, in the fundamentals, is in good condition. You do not have to redo the systems, you just have to repaint, you have to replace the sanitary and you have to change the floor in one of the rooms.

In light of my experience, I can tell you that the cost of the work is around $ 10,000.

We set a maximum ceiling of $ 8,000 and let us venture to IKEA.
To finance the operation, I stick to what all the books say about financial growth: select the mortgage which, among other things, is given you at a very low rate.
After all, we are taught by American gurus and local popularizers, in which other sectors we lend the money to 2-3%?

If you are an entrepreneur like me and sometimes you have come to the bank to ask for money, you know exactly what I am talking about.

The bank will finance 80% of the work because today 100% of mortgages are rare if you do not have a particular past history.

However, since we are good and credible, the bank also finances the work partly, so on $ 60,000 of spending we receive a loan of $ 48,000.

I tried to pull down estimates for a twenty-year mortgage and the lowest provides a monthly payment of $ 234.95 in 20 years, with costs of investigation of $ 850 and appraisal for $ 320

To this, you must add other additional expenses such as:

- Compulsory house cover: the annual cost that I estimate is about $ 240 which makes $ 4,800 for 20 years;
- Life insurance: bad luck aside, one can not be exposed to the risk of leaving debts to the heirs. I estimated a cost based on my age (27 years) and a capital of $ 50,000 I assure you with

about $ 80 per year ($ 1,600 total in 20 years) if you have a few years more than me you could pay a little 'more, put it in a quote;

- Disability coverage: make all the perils of the world here too, for me, safety comes first. I never went around with the scooter because I was afraid of falling, imagine if I buy a house with the risk of not having the money to make up for the diseases. Here, too, I made the estimate on myself and took out an annual cost of about $ 150, then $ 3,000 total over 20 years of a mortgage.

Calm, it's not over yet. At these expenses you must add:

- Real Estate Agency commission: on a purchase of this type you must estimate at least $ 3,500;
- Notarial deed: the costs are at your expense, you must pay both the deed of sale and the deed of loan, for the joy of the notary of the rogant. At least $ 4,000 are needed;
- Registry tax: in short, if you buy as a first home pay less but, as an investment, we must rule out

this hypothesis because you will not go there to live. The purchase, therefore, you do it as a second home and, therefore, pay the beauty of 9% that corresponds to $ 4,500.

To sum up, the total cost of the operation is:

- $ 56.388 (total to be returned to the bank) +
- $ 8,000 (furniture) +
- $ 850 (preliminary investigation) +
- $ 320 (appraisal) +
- $ 4,800 (home coverage) +
- $ 1,600 (life insurance) +
- $ 3,000 (disability coverage) +
- $ 3,500 (agency) +
- $ 4,000 (notary) +
- $ 4,500 (registration tax) = $ 86,958

Without going into the merits of what you have to pay right away and what instead extensions over time, the operation costs you $ 4,337.90 per year (total divided into 20 years of mortgage), ie $ 362.33 per month.

Now we calculate the expenses of your competence, ie those that you must take out of your pocket and immediately:

- $ 12,000 (advance 20%) +
- $ 8,000 (furniture) +
- $ 1,170 (appraisal and investigation) +
- $ 3,500 (real estate agency) +
- $ 4,000 (notary) +
- $ 4,500 (taxes) =
- $ 33,170 is the capital you need to start the operation.

Now that we have done the calculations on the expense, we come to the lease of the property.

We want to make it to students, so in the two-room apartment, we create two beds that we make at $ 350 each, for a monthly income of $ 700, which makes $ 8,400 gross annual income.

Let us simplify and pretend to rent without an agency, the costs charged to us are the dry coupon, which immediately declines 21% of the rent (which falls to 6.636 $) and cono and maintenance fees that, again to simplify, I esteem in $ 1,500 per year.

There is $ 5,136 net.

Considering the weighted annual cost, the net profit is $ 788.10 ($ 5.136 - $ 4.347.90).

You are awake, however, and you have taken out the loan for the purchase, letting you lend the money from the bank.

In this case, the calculation on the return of the real estate investment must, therefore, be based on the actual return generated by your capital, net of the instalment to be paid to the bank.

Technically speaking we are talking about ROE, that is an acronym of Return On Equity, where "equity" is the Capital, that is the one that you pour from your own pocket.

The calculation of the ROE is done with this formula:

(Net Annual Income / Own Capital) * 100

We, therefore, calculate the Net Annual Income.

$ 5.136 - $ 2.819.40 (mortgage payment) - $ 470 (annual cost of insurance) = $ 1.846 annuity.

As for Capital Just you have spent $ 33,170 to start everything.

So if we put the data in the formula we find: (1.846 / 33.170) * 100 = 5.56%

Congratulations, you have earned 5.56% on your investment property and you did better than American government bonds that do not reach 2%.

Am I wrong or have you read something similar even in the newspapers?

Well, they're all false information and I'll explain why.

Investing in real estate: it is a profession, not an investment

As I begin to write this last paragraph I look at the clock: 2 hours have passed since I started to reckon.

It took 2 hours just to plan, I dare not imagine even the time it would take if I wanted to do it in practice.

If you are an entrepreneur or a professional you are used to reasoning according to the time value of your time, so just try to calculate the amount of hours needed to plan, organize and manage all this, which can generate (when and if all goes well) a income of around $ 2,000 per year.

And I have not even tried to imagine the value of income if, instead of going to the bank, I had bought with my own money.

At this point, you could tell me that my calculations are wrong because you would be able to cut many expenses and maximize profits.

Good boy. Compliments. Welcome to the entrepreneurs' world.

The difference between an investment and a business activity lies in the time it takes. I invest my money to make it work for me, I can even help a professional who drives me but, basically, I do not use 50, 100 or 200 hours per year to follow my investments.

If you take all this time to pursue an investment, you are an industry professional or an entrepreneur and you are working exactly as I am now working on preparing this article.

Furthermore, and I stop, I have shown you the hypothesis in which the investment forecast is right.

The reality is clearly much more complex and often full of contingencies and (small or large) errors of assessment. With all the variables we have seen, the chances of loss are not so remote. Moreover, since this is a business activity in all respects, the risks are high, as they must justify the potentially high returns.

So I'm the one who's going to turn the question to you now.

Are you still sure that investing in brick is a safe and sound deal?

As you can see, once the fog blanket and the ham on the eyes have been removed, it is immediately clear that this is an operation that has its degree of complexity, as well as a certain amount of (right) risks.

As such, you must treat it in the same way you approach your work.

You have to spend time, a lot of time, to do your analysis, the checks, the calculations of the case and the resolution of the small problems that will inevitably arise.

Furthermore, you must also bear the burden of "entrepreneurial" risks linked to the particular dynamics of this type of market.
Having said that, we have seen that there are still opportunities, even if they have to be selected with greater attention and precision than in the past.

Chapter 4

10 More lessons about the real estate market

1. Understand the peculiarity of the real estate market

The "brick", as the real estate market was called fifty years ago, and as still calls it some nostalgic of the Sixties, is a market like any other. Remember: in finance, there is never a 100% safe investment! Each market has its own peculiarities, has its ups and downs and even the real estate market is a market that does not escape these logics. Investing in bricks can be useful and can offer interesting perspectives, but it is good that you first inform yourself before taking this step.

Do not limit yourself to looking at stock prices, but if you plan to buy an apartment or a box or another property, take a trip around the area. Consult the prices displayed outside the various real estate agencies in the district and compare them: often, even within the same city, prices change significantly from district to district. This happens because the costs of a real estate property are closely linked to the area in which it is built: if it is in the suburbs it will cost less than an exactly identical property but located in the city centre.

Furthermore, prices are also dependent on so-called connected services. For example: a three-room apartment has a certain cost if it is located in a condominium where there is a garden with its green care service by a specialized company, or there is a concierge service; an apartment with the exact same size but placed in a condominium without a green care service or porter will have a lower price.

2. Learn what is best to buy and what to stay away from

The very first choice that can be made, in terms of buying real estate as an investment, is certainly buying a small apartment - a studio or a two-room apartment, in short - that is located in a central area, well served by public transport and that has at least one connected parking space, if not a garage, and this would be the best solution. Why this advice?

A small apartment is much more easy to rent than a large one. Leasing an apartment to a family is very risky: you can go to cases of insolvency, and if there are children in the family, submit an injunction to eviction not only can be very complicated but you may not even be able to free your apartment. And so you would find yourself in the unpleasant situation of not being able to dispose of your personal assets and having to deal with insolvent tenants: they are two big problems, as you can imagine.

Instead, a studio or a two-room apartment can be rented to a professional who has moved to the city for work reasons. A person who does not have a dependent family but has a solid salary behind him is a guarantee of solvency and also, if the apartment you need or decide that it is time to resell it, you would have no difficulty in freeing it within the established time frame. If the studio can also combine a parking space - even if, we repeat, the box is the best solution - the added value of your property grows, especially if it is located in an area where parking can be a problem:

with a value added more, you can ask for a slightly larger rent. But you are still careful not to propose a fee outside of the logic of the market! You would risk never having a tenant, and then you would not even have an income.

Finally, a consideration on the location of the studio: central area and served by public transport. The central area because - usually - the city centres are lively areas, with rich proposals for both day and night life; but it is essential that there is also an excellent public transport service in the proximity of your apartment so that future tenants, if they do not want to use the car for movements, would still have the opportunity to go anywhere.

3. **Studying other real estate opportunities**

The box is a very interesting alternative to a standard one room apartment. First of all, the costs of a box are much, much smaller than those of an apartment, and this is definitely an advantage. Even if there were extraordinary condo fees in the complex where your garage is located, the rates for you would be very low, because proportionate to the small number of thousandths of which you are the owner. Moreover, when buying a box you should not worry about expenses related to the makeover and upholding of the domestic systems nor should you worry about restructuring or upgrading costs of sorts.

And then, if you make the smart choice to buy a box in an area where there is a lot of parking, you may have a very high probability of renting it. And not only that: you could find tenants very quickly, the replacement would be guaranteed in a very short time. Last but not least, the purchase of a box provides for a lower initial expenditure than that of an apartment: this means that, by renting it, you would be more quickly covered in expenses incurred.

4. **Always look for the right deal and not the right property**

Many investors in real estate investments are influenced by their feelings. Property is not money. You can see it, touch it, you can like it or not and all this affects our taste, our feelings precisely, going to compromise what our brain would say instead. To be able to be objective we must detach from the building and we must focus on our real goal, the deal. We must estrange from the property itself and look at all the economic aspects (cost, estimated costs of maintenance, condominium costs, classification value and cadastral income that affect taxes, commercial compatibility of the property and the area in which it is located in its market), it is clear that a beautiful property in a beautiful area can affect our senses more than a sad apartment in a suburban area, but often in suburban residential areas can be obtained at low costs, excellent profits, and continuity. Sometimes we strive to be objective but when we fall in love with something that objectivity fails without us even realizing it, it is at this moment that the role of our real estate consultant (that brings us back to the reality of the business, making us awaken from that 'falling in love) can be decisive preventing us from making a mistake that could cost us a bad deal.

5. **The income from a building must be seen in the continuity of the long term**

Sometimes when assessing the profitability of a property you look only at the maximum peak that the property can make without taking into account the time needed to make that property profitable.

Let's take a classic example, small property in a highly

residential area of high value, clearly it is a building that can produce a high return and many dwell only on this without taking into account the fact that it is a property that can be used for short periods giving long breaks in which the income becomes a cost (tax, condominium), it is necessary time or costs (of real estate agencies) to get that income and can also be incurred more often than the maintenance costs in addition to risking more easily the problematic situations or arrears that, although kept under control with the right tools, lead at least to an increase of time to devote to the problem (if not incurred expenses or lost revenue).

6. The real estate deal is made at the time of purchase and not of sale

Those who can buy with a substantial discount will never make mistakes. It may not be the most easily marketable building on the market, but when you have a substantial margin to sell it, everything becomes much simpler, safer and more profitable.

On the contrary, those who buy without getting a good discounted deal, that is at market price, counting on the fact that the market will rise, can easily find themselves in an uncomfortable position, given that even in a situation like the current one where prices are low and is actually the time to buy to do business, certainties about a further downturn or a safe short-term recovery do not exist, while those who buy below cost have the certainty of being able to resell at least the market price that would allow them to make a profit (which if then the market goes up can become an exceptional profit).

But at this point, the question is *how do you buy at a discounted price?* The answer is simple, you must look (and the market is always full of them, but especially in times of crisis like these) for a motivated seller, or someone who wants to sell, who no longer wants to keep that property, for any given reason. It is useless to waste time with someone who has obviously time or money and wants to make the maximum profit. On the other hand, you should always look for (and how many there are around today!) someone who does not have time and maybe even money. It will certainly be a motivated seller and ready to buy with a substantial discount your real estate deal.

7. **Learn how to set up and conduct a negotiation**

There are various factors ranging from experience and skills in the industry: from personal attitude (it's a bit like the good poker player who must have innate qualities to be able to bluff and bring his opponent straight to the goal that has been set, and other qualities that will instead refine with time and experience) to coldness and impartiality with respect to the affair.

It is clear that a good consultant will have all these characteristics being an expert who knows the techniques to be used in a negotiation, for example, a simple but always effective rule to follow is to never say a price first. It is statistically proven that the first to make a price by discovering, even if partially, their cards will eventually have a good chance of making the worst deal. The same building may be worth very different prices that depend fundamentally on the specific negotiating position of the parties and the respective ability to know how to conduct a negotiation. But a good consultant will also have the enormous advantage over the counterpart (and the investor represented) to be a third party, cold compared to the property and the deal, ready to lose the property and even the deal (if the deal no longer detecting oneself) without those guilt and loss senses that strike those who are about to reach the coveted object and suddenly see it slip out of hand (a certain element that often leads one of the parties when in negotiation personally to give up at a point or memento that will cost him inexorably a large part or all of his own profit), without considering that the third party consultant will have more chances to influence the counterpart towards his own objective of the part that will always be seen as an antagonist.

8. **Being able to buy without or with very little money and zero risk**

The most substantial real estate profit is always without costs. With huge advantages compared to investing with money. So always buy with as little money as possible, or even better, without your own money.

Do you have a bank fund? Of course it is possible, but unless you are in relationships or positions such that the lenders offer you easy money at very low costs or conditions, which happens in very few cases for very few categories of investors, the Banks, for costs and conditions imposed, are the worst way to get the necessary money for your investment.

The solution is to charge your real estate investment to three different parties, either alternatively or cumulatively. The first is a subject interested in living in the building, a formula that is increasingly successful is the rent with redemption, a form of atypical contract (which with the use is, however, being typed) that mixes lease and sale. Imagine finding a seller who, in order to get rid of the property, is willing to rent it with a redemption (today as there are always more rumours given the spread of the phenomenon and the difficulty of selling otherwise). We could propose a similar formula but more advantageous (fiscally) to this seller, we imagine proposing a preliminary contract with a payment in instalments (at three years if we want more transcription if we are not interested in transcribing), the seller accepts (becoming, in fact, our second investor) attracted by the possibility of getting rid of the property (or at least to forfeit the deposit after three years) and above all to get rid of expenses and of the real estate taxation that belongs to the owner, we investors do not spend a dollar: we limit ourselves to finding a tenant (the one who pays our real estate investment) that occupies the property. You deliver the money to be transferred to the owner in instalment as a deposit (as well as advance on the price), and at the end of the three years (or longer period agreed), we will have (without having spent a single dollar) the possibility of buying a property whose price has already been partially paid with that deposit actually paid by the tenant, now being able to evaluate if in the past years the market is climbed and the property has been appreciated or not we will have 3 possibilities abstractly verifiable:

1. the market has grown and the property has appreciated. We hypothesize a property for which at the time was agreed on the price of 500 thousand dollars of which 50 thousand already paid in the form of instalment, we imagine that the property is worth 600 thousand today we can pay it 450 thousand (or we can offer the purchase, if we do not have money available to a financing partner, third party that could finance our real estate investment, which paying it in full or in part

based on its real value of 600 thousand allows us to conclude an excellent profit, with certainty and without risk our money if not at the end and minimally).

2. The market has remained stable, so in our example, the property is still worth 500 thousand but we will pay 450 thousand, being a part already paid by our tenant. In this case, however, we will have made a good profit, although not as exceptional as in the previous case.

3. The market has dropped a lot. It is the worst case scenario in which if we had invested our money we would have made a substantial loss or we should keep the property locked for years waiting for better times, but with our strategy, we can decide not to buy the property, without losing anything, the deposit will, in fact, be paid by our tenant and we were able to exit at no cost from the worst situation that could happen, virtually eliminating risks and losses.

The exemplified use of the preliminary contract and the deposit is only one of the many examples that explains how the knowledge of contracts and real estate tax that every real good real estate consultant should know can bring a lot of value to the new investor.

9. Learn how to save money on the investment

At a time like this when the tax oppression has reached, in all sectors (and especially in the real estate industry), a very high level, the result of any investment can never reach (except in exceptional cases) the return that can be guaranteed by significant tax savings. So if the real estate profit that I can go to realize can also be halved by the weight of the tax, it is clear that I, if I find the way to avoid that tax oppression (or at least reduce it enormously), I can have a higher profit. So the golden rule is to find the way to adopt those contractual-tax measures (and there are really dozens of atypical contracts usable in this regard) that can, through the tax lever, double your real estate profit

10. **You do not have to be an expert to get returns on your real estate investments**

Very true. In fact, Warren Buffett is not an expert in real estate, let alone is an expert in farms or shopping centres. So how did you invest and achieve these results even if you are not an expert? The reason is simple. Warren Buffett knows the rules of investments and applies them in all fields: on the stock exchange, in real estate, in the business. Warren Buffett knows how to recognize an investment opportunity, take action and close a big deal.

That is why even a person who is not an expert in real estate can invest and earn a lot: because you do not need to be an expert, but you must know the rules of the game, or the basis of investment, and these can be learned by anyone, even from those who do not believe it is possible to learn them. The next step is then to put these notions and strategies into practice. The result? You will get results, just like Warren Buffett has been doing for decades. Not a bad perspective, right?

Chapter 5

Should you buy a house?

S hould you buy a house today? This is the first question that we will try to answer in this chapter.

Today, probably, is the best time to buy a house: according to the numbers we used to write the books, in fact, the price of real estate has been declining for some time: December 2017 has marked yet another minimum peak, since the average price of real estate dropped to $1944 per square meter.

Since this is a trend that has been going on for some time, I do not exclude that it can continue even if, according to the information that I have collected in recent years, it may have almost reached the bottom and be ready for a reversal.

So basically, if you have money available now, it may be the best time to buy a home at a low price.

The fact that it is worth starting to think about buying is supported by the national data, that have shown a good recovery during 2016 and 2017.

The latest data provided by the Nomisma observatory speak of a growth of 16% in 2016 (final data).

The recovery of the brick, as Nomisma says, is not uniform throughout America as it mainly characterizes cities such as New York and Los Angeles, where short-term rentals are driving the market. In the end, Central America is where the market continues to stagnate.

Rent or mortgage?

I will now try to answer the usual question: should you rent or take out a mortgage? I estimated a family with two income of 2500 dollars a month in total buying a property of 100 thousand dollars, asking for a fixed rate loan of 80 thousand dollars (80% of the amount) to be repaid in 20 years.

The estimate is based on the district of New York and I consider to have a well rounded knowledge about a mortgage. The average monthly payment is about $390.

Consider that, in addition to the mortgage, on a property of 100 thousand dollars you must consider:

- Mediation of the real estate agency: the cost for a flat of this kind varies between 3 thousand and 4 thousand dollars;
- Notary: to register the act of purchase and the loan, approximately 4 thousand dollars are required;
- Registration tax: if you buy as a first home it is 2% of the value of the property if it is your second home you pay 9%. Let's assume it is the first home, the cost is 2 thousand dollars;

To facilitate the calculation, I do not take into account other expenses (furniture for example).

In a nutshell, if you want to buy an apartment worth 100 thousand dollars you must have at least 20% of the amount (20,000 dollars) along with other expenses that are equal to about 10 thousand dollars. Total expenses to be incurred immediately: around 30 thousand dollars.

We now come to the analysis of the advantages and disadvantages.

Advantages
- The property finished paying, is yours. The best investors in the world would question this advantage, but since most people think it is a good thing to have a property, let me put it in the advantages section. Whether it is useful to possess something or not, it is up to you to decide;
- Rental money is almost totally "lost" and the rental price has been reduced less than the house prices;
- A house will be modeled as you like: it is yours and you can do whatever you like with it.

Disadvantages

- With today's precariousness, making a 20-year mortgage means exposing yourself to risks such as loss of work. The banks do not think twice, in case of insolvency, to throw you out;

- Once you buy a house it will be very difficult to get out of it. It will also be up to you to do cyclical works of extraordinary administration which, being rented, you do not have to bear as it is taken care of by the owner;

- While you are paying the house you have to pay the bank but, for the state, it is already yours: you are therefore required to pay all taxes on the house even if you have still not finished paying it.

How to buy a home with real estate leasing

In recent years, real estate leasing for individuals has been affirmed. Until now we have known leasing, as individuals, to buy the car: now, however, thanks to the recent intervention of the government, the possibility has also been introduced for the purchase of properties for private individuals.

The prescribed formula is particularly disciplined and is considered as an alternative to rent, mortgage and rent with redemption.

In two words, let me explain the real estate leasing: the bank buys the property and the customer takes possession of it by paying a rent (which can be at a fixed or variable rate) periodically.

From the beginning of the operation, the price of the possible redemption is contractually fixed: at the end of the leasing plan, whose duration is between 12 and 20 years, the customer can buy a house paying the final maxi-payment.

Are there any tax breaks?
The answer is yes, especially for young couples. According to the recent Stability Law, in fact, people under 35 with an annual income of no more than 55 thousand dollars can deduct from 19 per cent each year up to a maximum of paid fees of 8 thousand dollars (therefore, with a calculator in hand, the maximum sum deductible is 1,520 dollars).

For the over 35 years, however, the facility is different but still considerable as it works exactly like the one currently established for the first home loan.

In this case, therefore, 19% of the leasing fee can be deducted up to 4 thousand dollars (the maximum deductible each year, therefore, is 758 dollars).

What changes fiscally between leasing and taking out a mortgage?

The significant difference between leasing and a mortgage concerns the fact that the lease on which to calculate the 19% tax exemption is given by the full amount of the fee paid to the bank while on the mortgage, as is known, only affects the interest installment amount.

Let's try to make an example. If James in one year has paid on a mortgage installments equal to 6 thousand dollars and of these 6 thousand we specify that 4 thousand represent the principal amount and 2 thousand the interest rate, in the calculation of the income tax deduction related to the first home loan, equal to 19%, is calculated on 2 thousand dollars. In the case of leasing, however, the deduction is based on the total rent.

Finally, for the real estate leasing, another tax advantage is provided that concerns the final maxi-payment.

By redeeming the property for payment of the maxi-installment contractually fixed in principle, in fact, it is possible to deduct 19% of a maximum amount of 20 thousand dollars from the national tax.

If to be clear, to redeem the house I add 30 thousand dollars, you can deduct from the national tax 3,600 dollars or 19% of the 20 thousand dollars that represent the maximum deductible. I will personally closely monitor the evolution of this new opportunity and evaluate the impact it will have on the market. Are you looking for advice on making real estate investments and are you wondering if this is the right time to make profitable real estate investments in America?

In this chapter, you will find some useful advice for your investments and some tips on mistakes not to commit, as well as an analysis of the situation in the real estate market today.

2018 could be a good year to take the big step: whether the idea is to buy a property to live there or to make a real estate investment, the trend of the market and, in general, of prices seems to suggest that we are in a positive phase from this point of view to find bargains at reasonable prices.

Many have understood it, so much so that according to data released by the Nomisma observatory, there is a more sign regarding the purchase of apartments to be used for residential purposes.

The real estate market, it is good to underline it in the opening, in addition to being schizophrenic, varies from area to area: very often, even within the same city, the trends are very different.

I appeal to a varied audience, so I base my analysis on general data concerning our country: the particular case, therefore, could be totally different from the general reasoning that I illustrate. It is not a mistake, I must necessarily simplify some concepts because, being the local market very local, I can not know the exact situation of each district of each city.

This article, in essence, is aimed at those who want to buy a house to make an investment and not to live there: on this issue, there are many other guides, first on the whole general about buying the house that I advise you to read.

Among the various solutions to the purchase, moreover, you could evaluate the prospect of real estate leasing if you are looking for a viable alternative to the classic mortgage.

I repeat the concept not to misunderstand: in this page, we talk about investments in bricks, not residential sales.

Making an investment property means buying a property to put it into income by renting it or to sell it in better times.

The data and advice that you find in the next paragraphs, therefore, should be read in this light.

Advice for investing in the real estate market in a secure manner

Before going on to examine in more detail the general framework of today about the real estate market and its trend, I would like to provide you with some tips for investing in brick.

We know that, until at least a few years ago, we Italians have always had the dream of investing in brick, as this form of investment has always seemed the best way to invest and make savings.

However, this kind of market no longer offers the security of once and this is not always easy to understand when and if buying a home can be a real deal.

Below you will find some suggestions to understand if real estate investments are safe and if it is better to buy a house, especially if it will not be the residence, but a real investment.

1. Study a neighborhood/area thoroughly

Deciding to examine and "specialize" on a particular district of a city, or on an archipelago of adjacent countries, can be the winning weapon to capture in advance the property that deserves to be purchased and become the source of your investment.

Studying an area involves knowing the type and target population that lives there, the types of housing that we find located, the prices of the same.

It is essential to know everything about the area of interest, as this is the right way to understand when we are facing an opportunity.

On this page, you can follow the market trends in the main Italian cities. Furthermore, on My Business, you will find two in-depth articles dedicated to Milan and Rome.

2. Buy a rented apartment
Buying an accommodation or a property that is already inhabited by someone who has rented allows

you to count on a lower price than what we could find for a house that is empty, despite the square footage is the same: we even speak of a decline in price equal to about 25%, which will be recovered when the accommodation will be emptied, when the current tenants decide to leave.

If the tenant present in the house has already given solvency tests over the years, moreover, it eliminates the breakage of boxes to have to carefully select who will pay the monthly fee: these days, given the Italian legislation, it is certainly not a bad.

3. The bare ownership
Like the speech just made, even buying the bare property can be an excellent investment, as the house remains accustomed by the current tenant (the usufructuary), but for this reason, the value of the property can go down very significantly and it can be treated.

Buying bare ownership implies that at the time of the decease of the usufructuary tenant, the house will regain its full value and, obviously, the heirs of the deceased will have no right on the building itself.

4. Attention to the price per square meter!
Did you know that in larger cities, larger houses cost less per square meter than smaller homes?

This means that the smaller buildings must be kept in check, also because small houses are more in demand, both in the suburbs and in the city centers.

Obviously, when making an investment of this type, it is very important to understand if the area is well served or if it could be diveltarlo: find a property in an area near urban redevelopment can cost less, and buy value once the process of improvements in the neighborhood.

Always check this information and make sure that the interventions are really done: remember that we are in Italy, not in Switzerland!

5. Choose the best phase to buy
Another fundamental advice is to evaluate very

carefully the moment in which to complete the sale.

Being aware of the current phase of the real estate cycle is essential to conclude a deal, because, during periods of recession, prices fall, because it is more difficult to sell and it is more important, for those who really want to sell, do it quickly, maybe just to counter the various problems related to the cyclical recession.

In the phases in question prices are lowered, while the number of houses to choose from increases. Remember that!

6. To reckon not to make mistakes
You have spotted a house whose value can not increase significantly in the long run, but do you like it anyway and want it at all costs?

Before signing, check that it can be rented at a gross annual rent of at least 5% of the total investment value (if it were higher it would be even better, according to some experts the ideal is 10%), which is equal to the purchase price of the house (+ the fees for the real estate agent, the restructuring costs, if any, and the costs required to carry out the relevant notary practices).

7. Buy residential and non-commercial properties
Preferring residential properties is better than choosing commercial ones, which may perhaps seem more convenient for a profit, but which require different and in a certain sense more complex requirements, as well as in the case of land.

Better not to complicate your life!

8. Find sellers who are motivated
It may seem out of place to try to understand who you are dealing with and who is the one selling you the house? Instead, it could help in the conclusion of a deal.

In fact, dealing with someone who has a certain concern to sell (perhaps because he must use the proceeds to buy) could be more profitable than having to deal with a subject that has many houses to sell and can afford to wait.

9. Negotiate

The art of negotiation can be useful: the first trick is to never export first by saying a price that you intend to pay.

The risk that it is to the advantage of your interlocutor, who perhaps expected a less advantageous exchange.

If you then think you can get a little more trying at least try: you could make your deal even cheaper with a little 'persuasion!

10. The offer must be made in writing

To avoid unpleasant incidents, write all the agreements on special forms that you can find online or at real estate agencies: avoid verbal agreements, even if you know the person in front of you.

11. Be careful not to get lost!

Keep in mind that when you buy a property, often you

consider only the profitability, and never the maintenance costs, taxes and the various contingencies that we may encounter.

For this reason, I suggest you be realistic and evaluate every expense so that your purchase is an investment and not an error.

Do not miss even one of the points listed above and you will not regret!

12. Real estate = income? Not always...
Although the tourist area may seem like a profitable and profitable deal, suitable for spending money and investing in brick, this is not always the case.

Above all, if you live somewhere else, consider that if you opt for this geographical choice, you would have a trusted person on site, able to support you with various paperwork and not related to the management of the house and the rent of tourists.

Moreover, the prices of tourist resorts are often inflated by other constraints that cause prices to rise and make investments unprofitable.

I give you an example on a place that I know personally: I was born in a small village on the Amalfi Coast, despite the speculative bubble of the Sixties has unfortunately devastated the aspect of the country, it falls like all the territory under the protection of UNESCO and there are a myriad of landscape constraints that prevent the construction of new houses.

It is easy to understand that a seaside resort, a stone's throw from Amalfi, has an extremely strong market due to the demand for tourist rentals. The entire economy is based on tourism, so much so that many property owners over the years have become hoteliers starting B & B activities or simply renting houses through portals like AirBNB.

And internal demand? Obviously, the locals want to buy a house to live there, there are no new buildings and existing ones already have a high value given the tourist flows.

The result is that today, to buy a central or semi-central building, we need a figure ranging from 4,500 to 5,000 € per square meter: 100 square meters cost half a million dollar.

The yield of a house of this type leased in the summer months can reach a maximum of 30,000 dollars (just 3% of the value of the property) from which you must subtract the costs of maintenance, management, and taxes.

Ah, yes ... there are those who think to live again in the eighties and thick to black but I strongly discourage you!

13. Being Goals is fundamental
Try to be objective in evaluating the property you have in front of you: if you lose your reason in front of a beautiful veranda, you may not realize that the property is exposed to the north and that the mold is ready to make its appearance, even if carefully hidden from the seller!

If you neglect some more or less important details you

may notice too late that the value of the property has been compromised by the slices of ham that you put before your eyes.

You are investing, you are not buying the house of your dreams ... even if it were, be careful!

14. Invest in solitude
What does it mean? I advise you, if you can afford it, to invest alone, and not in cooperation with a friend or relative: certainly, this will lead you to avoid any future annoyances!

Prevention is better than cure, always!

15. Investing abroad is convenient?

Are you going to buy a property abroad? As in the case of the house in the tourist area, remember that you may have more stomach ache because of the distance between your home and the one you would like to rent.

If however, you intend to do so, try to keep in mind the risk that you may have additional risks such as those related to a currency exchange if you want to buy out of the dollar zone.

In these extra-EU cases, it is good to keep in mind that a house bought abroad with another currency can be subject to changes that can lead to losses.

After seeing 15 basic tips, our analysis continues.

Forecast on the resumption of the real estate market
Now that we have given some ideas that can be inspiring, I would like to propose a more detailed analysis of the actual convenience, or otherwise, that this kind of investment can have, examining the real estate market and its recent trend, so as to help you read the current picture and understand if this investment is for you.

The data that you find below are the national ones of the known portale Immobiliare.it.

In the last 24 months in Italy, the price per square meter has dropped dramatically, we have analyzed it in depth also in the deepening dedicated to the price trend city by city.

The economic crisis and the credit crunch of the banks have influenced this not a little. In the meantime, we are updating in August 2017: the value of real estate continues to fall inexorably, although perhaps less dramatically than in the recent past.

Despite the declining prices for years, however, between 2015 and 2016, the sales are spread and even 2017-2018 should continue on this trend.

We must not be fooled by the idea that the recession is over: simply those who had money have waited and "baptized" this period as the most profitable time to develop profitable real estate investments.

We must also add another non-secondary passage that is also apparent from the study cited above: the possibility of buying a house for Italians is subject to the granting of a loan by a bank.

Therefore, the wealth of consumers has not increased,

but it is banks that have resumed lending, especially thanks to the aid of quantitative easing launched by the ECB and that many would like to end as soon as possible.

If you want to invest in brick, then, this could be the right time for a series of favorable conditions:

- The real estate market goes to cycles and, in the long run, it always grows. The last peak was recorded in the middle of the first years of 2000, before reaching today's levels. For these heterogeneous situations today, or perhaps in a few months, we will touch the worst peak then, inevitably, prices will rise;

- Mortgages will increase in the next few years: this makes us think of the ECB's QE. The introduction of money by the dollarpean institutions aims to lower mortgage rates. In all probability they will resume loans at more affordable rates, so the demand for people ready to buy a house will increase. On the point, I recommend reading the article: Buy a house without money, invest in the brick without a mortgage;

- The timid signs of economic recovery could increase demand: where GDP should return to growth (spurred on by a series of questionable circumstances), it is inevitable that there will be more people willing to buy. The more there are, the clearer the price of the real estate will rise.

The mortgage: how is today an opportunity?
Let's deepen what was said now: when we talk about buying a house to go there to live strongly recommend the mortgage.

The main personal finance experts, in fact, believe that the house to be used as a home should not be bought but that is not what interests us here.

In the previous paragraph, you read that mortgages are disbursed at this stage with decidedly low rates.

If this could increase the number of potential buyers, it could also be an advantage for investors.

Buying a house involves an investment of a good amount of liquidity, it may be useful to think about taking a part of the money also considerable to mortgage (it can be up to 80% usually) by exploiting the very low rates. If you want to know it yourself, click here to make a quick quote.

Obviously, the financing, if adequately spread over time, would be paid by the tenants who monthly match the rent.

What does this mean?
That for example with 12 thousand dollars of your own pocket you could buy a property of 60 thousand dollars financed for the remaining 48 thousand dollars from the mortgage (in turn paid through the rent charged which, insured before, must be higher than the installment you owe correspond to the bank).

Given the long-term uptrend in rental rates, mainly due to inflation but also to the labor mobility that characterizes our era, you may find yourself after a few years to receive a higher rent with the mortgage that, in case of fixed rate, remains the same in the amount of installments but, in fact, "weighs" less.

Obviously, you have to have a series of requirements to obtain a mortgage and the credibility that you have towards the bank is generally essential to access the credit: if you are thinking of investing in the brick, then, do not underestimate this aspect!

The considerations expressed make us believe that 2018 is the good year for a real estate investment in Italy or at least to start thinking about it.

Prices continue to fall despite the economy's showing signs of recovery and banks seem intent on keeping mortgage rates low.

I can not say when we will touch the lowest point - also in light of the fact that each city has a different story - but we can assume that, in the next five years, a slight increase in apartment prices can not be ruled out.

The best solutions, if you decide to buy, seem to be buying in areas close to universities or in tourist places to rent with a temporary contract.

Since there is greater "volatility" in the tenants, the continuous replacement and the average higher economic conditions of those who stay should give some more guarantees than renting in a residential area.

Another really interesting path can be represented by solutions like the one offered by Uniplaces, which aims precisely at this specific target.

If you really want to invest in a residential area, do so on medium-high-end properties leased to people able to provide adequate financial guarantees.

All this, of course, can not ignore the consideration that nowadays nothing is more indefinitely and it is not to be excluded that a worker with all the papers in good standing in a few years, unfortunately, may no longer be able to pay.

Investing always involves risks and this is also the case when the object of the investment is brick.

Chapter 6

A concrete example

Every time I talk about money, inevitably the speech falls on the theme of real estate: buying a house is a little bit in the head of us Italians, however, we tend to make confusion between the purchase for residential use and the concept of investment property that is all ' else.

If you are reading this article it is very likely that at least once in your life you will have the problem of investing in the brick or that the thing, in any case, will fascinate you.

Wealth, moreover, tends to manifest itself in material goods: how many times have you thought of a person who you think is rich, or at least well-off, and you have started mentally to rebuild its real estate and land?

Come on, if you were born in a small country like me, you surely know the few locals who are considered rich and know exactly how many apartments they have and how many cars have matriculated in recent years.

However, the concept of wealth in terms of real estate assets or "tangible" assets does not always coincide with financial wealth, which is quite another. I tell you frankly to remove the equation "so many houses = so much wealth" that often lies in the head of my interlocutors.

This article is born with a specific goal: it is the best in-depth analysis on the web that deals with the matter of real estate investments.

A real analytical guide that tells you when it is better to buy a house to make an investment by asking you specific cases.

I decided to write this fundamental guide after years of study during which I read many books on the subject, I observed the market of two locations that I know following the price trend and personally viewing dozens of properties.

A universal method

The numbers that you report may not correspond exactly to your area, I tell you to avoid misunderstandings because the real estate market is influenced by strongly local dynamics, but you can use the scheme that I report in the next few lines to make a calculation and evaluate the convenience of the area where you live or where you are interested in operating.

The prices you see may also vary for the sample cities: I calculated based on the situation updated in August 2017 based on the average current prices and mortgage rates for the period.

Little note on the estimate of costs: on some steps you may not find yourself because I decided to simplify not considering the credit mediation (many do not receive the loan directly from the bank but rely on an external mediator). Other simplifications can be found on the estimate of mortgage costs that vary depending on the bank lending, the historical period and the economic situation of the applicant.

The purpose is not to calculate the exact mortgage payment or to tell you exactly what is left in your pocket but I want to provide you with a method.

Thanks to this article, in fact, you will be able to have in mind an operational map with which you can evaluate in 10 minutes when and if it is convenient to move: in many cases, I assure you, you should stay and watch.

Practical Guide to Real Estate Investments
After having done all the premises of the case, we enter the concrete analysis that you must print and use as a bible before investing in real estate.

I chose to do a simulation based on two cities that I know:

turin
It 's the city where I live now, my simulation is focused on the San Paolo district where I live and set up on the purchase of a two-room apartment of about 50 square meters to be rented to students who come to the city to study at the Polytechnic.

If the city fascinates you, I have also written a general guide for those who want to move. Turin can be a good example if you want to invest a large city because most of its features are common to all large urban areas.

Maiori (SA)

Maiori is my country of origin where I lived for 25 years. Located on the Amalfi Coast, it is in a strategic position because it is close to the most famous Amalfi, Positano, and Ravello and represents a typical tourist resort that can be taken as an example for those who want to make a real estate investment to be monetized with short rentals for vacationers.

Now I will explain to you analytically the method I used to do my calculations, prepare to take notes because no one has ever told you freely what you are about to read.

Hypothesis # 1 - Turin

As mentioned, my hypothesis is based on the purchase of a property located in the San Paolo district, a strategic area because very close to the Polytechnic University of Turin and ideal for rent to students as less expensive than the area immediately closer to the University.

The area is well served by public transport and is commercially alive, much of the neighborhood is inhabited by families, the elderly, workers or students and the rental market is good both because it is oriented to the out-of-office flows that come to study in Turin that to the flows of workers who move to the city.

The price per square meter at the time of writing the first version of this article (August 2017) varies from € 1000 for properties to be restored up to € 1800 for properties in good condition. Recently, for completeness of information, I saw new apartments for sale just built at a price of 2200 dollars per square meter.

We estimate to be good negotiators and to be able to identify a two-room apartment to be renovated that we are priced at € 50,000.

The building, as regards the fundamentals, is in good condition: you do not have to redo the systems, you just have to repaint, replace the sanitary and you have to change the floor in one of the rooms. Without wanting to exaggerate, we estimate an expense for the works of € 10,000.

The property must be furnished, even here we do not go too far (Ikea, Mondo Convenienza, etc are our allies!) And set a ceiling of € 8,000.

If we want to make a serious investment, the golden rule is to use the leverage of the loan.

Many have told you that making the mortgage is bullshit: in fact, the concept applies to the home property because it is as if you were buying consumer goods in installments. But this is not the point, when you make an investment it is essential that you use the debt lever because it allows you to limit the disbursements you have to sustain and make your operation sustainable in the long term: if you do well the accounts, in fact, the mortgage the tenant pays you for it.

In what other market do you lend your money at 2-3% per year? This only happens in real estate, if you have a company and have tried to apply for a loan for your business, you understand perfectly what I am talking about.

At this moment in time, no bank will lend you more than 80% of the sum needed: the bubble burst in 2008 put an end to the easy credit season and the banks are trying to learn the lesson.

Let's assume all the requirements to receive the loan and we estimate to exploit the leverage as much as possible: the bank will lend us 80% of the sum needed for the purchase and we will finance the work to 80% (this second hypothesis, however, it depends on several factors: not all banks are willing and, above all, it also depends on your economic situation and your payer history!).

To sum up: 50,000 + 10,000 = 60,000 dollars total, 80% of which corresponds to 48,000 dollars.

The mortgage also requires additional unavoidable

expenses: the expertise, which you can have from one of your assessors or one sent by the bank (to simplify, let the bank charge you on the loan) and the costs of preliminary investigation and opening of the practice. We estimate these costs in around € 1,500 to be added to the sum seen previously.

Chapter insurance. In reality, the only compulsory insurance is the one on the house, but I'll tell you one thing: do not be grumpy on this point.

The bank, of course, will try to sell you everything but in my opinion, it is essential to have:

4. Compulsory housing coverage - the Estimated annual cost of 50 square meters in Turin of € 240 which makes € 4,800 for 20 years;
5. Coverage life - It is fundamental, what would happen to your heirs if I failed? It also touches iron and you make all the spells but the problem remains, better to make sure. I estimated a cost based on my age (27 years) and a capital of € 50,000 I assure you with about 80 € per year (€ 1,600 total in 20 years) if you

have a few years more than me you could pay a little 'more;

6. Disability coverage - Even here, you do all the spells in the world but they are things that can happen. Is it better to pay a few hundred dollars more per year or is it better to break the boxes to relatives and people who are close to you and hope for the help of the INPS? The ideal would be that the unseemly situation never occurs, however, statistically, it can happen. The estimate made on myself has brought out an annual cost of about € 150 which make € 3,000 total over 20 years of a mortgage.

In summary, given that the bank generally charges the policies and expenses on the loan, the total amount of the loan will be: 48,000 + 1,500 + 1,600 + 4,800 + 3,000 = € 58,900.

We now come to the calculation of interests: in this historical moment, it is possible to tear a fixed rate to 2.5% finite (the rate is calculated by adding the 3-month Euribor and the spread, ie the cost applied by the bank).

We use a known mortgage comparator to calculate the final installment. The result is € 16,007 of interest that you must add to the original sum.

Then:

€ 58,900 + € 16,007 = € 74,907 total to be repaid over 20 years.

Location of the building

The purpose is to exploit the students who come to Turin, in the two-room apartment you can get two beds that, average hypothesis, allow you to get € 350 per student for a total of € 700 per month. Our gross income is € 8,400 per year.

To simplify, let's pretend to rent the house alone without an agency: if we buy a single house and live in the city we can manage if we aim to own many properties it becomes really difficult not to make use of mediation.

From this money, however, we must take away the dry coupon: the law sets it at 21% for the free rent, in some cities can apply to 10% but we must stick to the prices set by the municipality. To simplify, we estimate 21%, so our € 8,400 becomes € 6636.

At this point we subtract about 1,500 € per year that will be allocated to pay the condo fees, taxes and extra charges (it counts that even if you have just done the work, sooner or later you will still need to repair something that can break, so ideally consider that a 40-50% of this 1,500 € per year must serve to cover these eventualities even if they do not physically take them out immediately).

To summarize: € 6636 - € 1,500 = € 5.136 to which you have to subtract € 3,745.32. In total you remain:

€ 1390.68 net income corresponding to a net monthly income of € 115.89.

This is the economic result of the estimate. For financial assessments I refer you to the next paragraphs, now we also do the example relating to the purchase of the property in a tourist resort and then collect the sums jointly.

Hypothesis # 2 - Maiori (SA)

As anticipated, in this second hypothesis we speak of a tourist resort. Maiori is a strategic country on the Amalfi Coast because it is not mainstream like the best known places but it is very close and, above all, has more space and therefore more real estate.

The town is well connected to the main places of interest by sea and, with some headache due to traffic, can be reached quite easily by car or public transport.

Maiori, moreover, has the largest beach on the Amalfi Coast (which in reality is not Rimini or Riccione, so do not expect miles of umbrellas and chairs) and attracts a mixed tourist clientele: many families from Campania or neighboring regions usually spend holidays and, in recent years, the foreign presence has strongly increased.

Low cost tourism has largely migrated to other destinations (Cilento, Calabria, Puglia, abroad), so those who can afford a holiday in Maiori are potentially medium-high spending.

Tourism lasts about 6 months, from April to October, so when you buy a house you have to think about renting it for about 180 days.

While in Turin it is aimed at annual contracts, here the spare part becomes much more frequent because a stay, on average, lasts 3-4 days.

There is the task, therefore, to live on site to follow arrivals and departures or it is necessary to delegate to others, so you have to budget this item of expenditure. In the example, to simplify, let's pretend that we deal with it and therefore we do not estimate this cost.

We come now to the market analysis. The price of real estate is decidedly different than in Turin, the range goes from € 3,500 per square meter for homes farther from the sea to € 6,500 for properties near the seafront, some houses are also sold at € 7-8000 per square meter in the presence of details comfort or strategic positions.

We estimate to be good and to be able to snatch a price per square meter of € 4,500 for a two-room apartment of 50 square meters that requires some work quantifiable at € 12,000.

The purchase price, therefore, is € 225,000 + € 12,000 of work.

For the furniture, we are good and effective and spend the same amount of Turin: € 8,000.

We are asking for a loan of 80% out of € 237,000 (price + work) that we spread over 30 years instead of 20 given the higher investment.

To the sum indicated we must add the related expenses that we have already seen in the Turin example:

Compulsory housing coverage - the Estimated annual cost of 50sqm which I calculated on the website of a well-known insurance company is € 109.50 per year (€ 3,285 in 30 years);
Life coverage - The same reflection is made in the first

example, by making a quick estimate by entering my data comes out a prize of € 205.20 annual equal to € 6,156 in 30 years. Remember that the capital to be insured is higher as the buildings cost more;

Disability coverage - I do not accept the analysis made for the two-room apartment to be bought in Turin. Also here I have included my personal data by taking out a quote on capital to be insured of more than € 377 per year which becomes € 11,310 in 30 years;

Bank charges - Expertise and other costs, even here we estimate € 1,500.

Lease of the building

Now we can move on to monetizing our purchase. I have friends who run vacation rentals in Maiori, the data that I provide them I ripped after having discussed with them for a long time.

In summary, the monthly return of a two-room apartment ranges from a minimum of € 2,000 in the low season to a maximum of € 4,000 in the high season. These are estimates, there are also homes that are located at € 1,500 or € 5,000, as always the truth lies in the middle.

Attention, I speak to you of gross return to which you have to subtract the rest. Unfortunately, Italy is full of cunning people who collect the money without declaring anything, I strongly advise you against black for a number of reasons:

you can not do it, respect the rules and stop the misery and always try to be smart;
the State, sooner or later, will present you with the bill: controls are increasing, the purchase of a property is a public fact and risks penalties higher than the gains you make;
managing a lot of cash is dangerous, most of the time you have to devote to "sorting" money that you can not pay into your current account you can use it to create other income-producing activities. Do you know only one developed country where it becomes blacker than Italy ?;
above all foreign customers pay by credit card. It 's just a matter of time and even we Italians who are always tardoni we will adapt, so the carousel is destined to run out.
Having said that, assuming to always fill for the six months of the summer season, the maximum

achievable yield is € 20,000. Maybe in October or in April, you can have some holes that fill with some tourist passing through November or February, I do not know if I give the idea, but we take this gross sum as maximum yield that can be achieved, the difference dances on a gap of 2-3 thousand dollars at most.

An unavoidable cost that you have is that of the laundry: at each stay, you have to find at least clean linen, you will not want to lose you for so little? From what I have reported, the cost is about € 6 per wash: considered 180 days of activity and 3.5 days average per stay, you have to wash the laundry for 51.50 times. In a nutshell: € 6 x € 51.50 = € 309. You can even wash your dirty clothes by yourself, but if you're thinking about investing it's not really ideal.

Cleaning chapter. If you do not want to do them personally, cleaning a 50 square meter apartment requires about 2 hours of work that cost about 20 dollars. Stays are € 51.50 x € 20 = € 1.030 is the cost you must bear.

Now, we take our rent of € 20,000 and subtract 21% of

the dry coupon (here I'll explain the operation of the coupon). 20,000 - 4,200 = € 15,800. The coupon pays the pay without being able to subtract the expenses because we are thinking like an investment from private, if I open VAT I would be slightly different but, in that case, we would go beyond the business and not the hard and pure investment.

From € 15.8000 we subtract € 309 + € 1030 which are the two items of expenditure that we have seen before: we are € 14.461.

In this case, too, we reserve around € 2,000 per year to be allocated to the condominium expenses, to additional taxes, and to any work, we have € 12.461.

Now it's the turn of the mortgage: € 12,461 - € 11,237.28 = € 1,223.72

€ 1,223.72 per year, which make € 101.97 net monthly income.

The economic result is not to be licked the mustache, I tell you for correctness that I overestimated the expenses at the time of purchase and I kept low on the margins, certainly it is a result that can be improved.

Both the examples I have drawn we need to get an idea, not to draw up a 100% detailed business plan.

Investment analysis

I preferred to group these reflections in a single paragraph, so as to evaluate both the situations I have illustrated so far.

I simplify two concepts, that of ROI (return on investment) and ROE (return on what you have actually invested in your pocket). The following is a simplified estimate, we would have to write the books on these two aspects but there are a number of experts who talk about it and you can investigate as best as you can to get school definitions. I am for the bread and salami that is raw but feeds you anyway, even in difficult situations.

ROI in practice measures the net gain as a percentage of ALL the capital invested, regardless of how much you have invested and how much money you have taken on debt. It is calculated by dividing the net gain for the capital allocated to its production multiplied by 100.

This is the reason why, in both cases, I calculated the total cost of the operation that does not take into account only the price of the property but all immediate and recurring expenses for the entire duration of the loan.

2. Two-room ROI in Turin: (€ 1390.68 net annual income / € 106,907 total expense) x 100 = 1.30%
3. Two-bedroom ROI in Maiori: (€ 1,223.72 net annual income / € 400,368 total expense) x 100 = 0.30%

The ROE is, as anticipated, the return on YOUR capital, that is on the money that you have actually pulled out to start the investment. In practice, it does not take into account the mortgage and the ancillary costs applied by the bank and loaded on the financing that will be borne, in the hypothesis that you always manage to rent, of your "customers".

The answer to the question: "Is it worth buying a house to invest?", So it's all here.

If you consider buying as a financial investment, forget it. Even by doing the simplest thing, that is, by investing in a deposit account, you can have similar or slightly lower net yields with a box break level of 0 or almost.

If, on the other hand, you start thinking about how to save costs and how to maximize revenue, instead, I welcome you to the entrepreneurs' club. You are not investing from a financial point of view, you are dedicating yourself to an economic activity, you are embarking on a business.

Chapter 7

Money Mindset to become a successful real estate wholesaler

In this chapter, we will go deep into the subject and discover the 30 golden lessons that every investor should know, before entering the stock market.

- **Easy money is like Santa Claus: it does not exist!**

Who promises to quintuple your assets without sweating is not more that a seller of smoke: investing in the stock market is not a joke and to achieve the investment goals you have set yourself to avoid risky securities, focusing on something more stable, lasting and profitable. In the recipe for success, in addition to a serious knowledge of the stock markets, there is also the sentimental component (for those investing there is no room for panic but a lot of patience) and even a bit of luck.

2. Gold and cash do not give interest

Everyone knows that cash does not disappear, but after the bizarre manoeuvrers of the European Central Bank (which brought negative returns on the single currency), we can be even more certain that investing in cash does not create any interest. The dream of all is to be able to accumulate that amount of money enough to enjoy a quiet retirement but the closer it gets to the time x, the more the small investor tends to panic. Hence the reckless choices to invest in cash or in commodities such as gold which, although it proves to be more stable than fiat, can not hold the same value forever. Just think that in the last lustre, the value of the most precious metal fell by 34.8%.

3. The ingredients for a winning strategy

One of the main factors of success on the stock exchange is sentiment: patience, foresight, and prudence are the three basic ingredients of winning strategies, but it is also true that a little risk never hurts.

If the money we have invested on a certain stock does not return, you should look around and find some slightly riskier but at least profitable activity, with the hope that an important injection of money into the markets can restart the economy by stimulating productivity and development.

4. Establish investment goals

Before starting to invest, then embark on a challenging and long path, you must have clear in mind where you want to go. It depends on personal aspirations, on the trust that one has for himself and on many other factors. However, the main choice is between protecting capital and making it grow. Under certain conditions, the stock exchange also lends itself to the speculative approach. Who wants to start could also establish concrete objectives such as buying a good or a service. In any case, the rule is always the same: to understand where you want to arrive.

5. Establish the degree of risk tolerance

This is probably the most important phase. The stock

market is in fact extremely varied and allows numerous approaches, from the prudent and static to the dynamic and courageous.

This is why it is always good to establish one's degree of tolerance. Based on this decision, further choices will be made, until the real investment is realized. Investor profiles depend on personal characteristics and their economic situation. If you are a simple worker, do not sail in gold and maybe those who invest are the savings of a lifetime, it is good to give up any speculative ambitions. The degree of tolerance determines the risk that you intend to run and the strategy that will be adopted later.

6. Studying

The information issue should not be forgotten. The stock market is complex, structurally risky, so we need to be cautious. The risk is to lose capital in a short period of time. Therefore, it is necessary to undertake a training course that confers at least the theoretical tools. The topic of the study should consist of both the investment modalities - how it is invested in the concrete - and the economic environment in general.

As for the sources, including paper texts, successful

books, and the internet, you are spoiled with choices.
The study activity, however, never abandons the investor, even when he has become an expert. Pressing is the need to update continuously, but also to inquire about everything that gravitates around the securities in the portfolio.

7. Choose the long term

Investing in the stock market should not be an activity of a few months or even a few years. It must be a continuous activity. It is only through patience and perseverance that it is possible to make substantial profits. This means that you need to build a long-term version, which looks at least for the next five years (even if ten are more suitable). This means that it is good not to give in to the temptation to sell the securities as soon as the prices start to fall. In the bag as in life is worth the saying "laugh well who laughs last".

8. Monitoring

If you opt for a long-term vision, as you should, then it is essential to monitor the status of your investment. Not everyone knows that control and monitoring begin before the investment itself. In particular, it is necessary to establish a benchmark, ie a yardstick by means of which it is possible to really understand whether we are on the right path or not. Finally, it is good to make a periodic comparison between the expected results and the real ones. At the beginning, there is a strong temptation to abandon oneself to discouragement, also because the results tend to arrive farther with time.

A general consideration can be made on the segment within which to operate. In fact, everything depends on risk tolerance. If this is very low, you should address those segments that by their nature do not suffer from the crisis. The reference is to those goods whose consumption is practically mandatory, therefore the food and pharmaceuticals. Investing in pharmaceutical companies' actions will not make you rich but is a very useful asset to protect capital. Strangely enough, but up to a certain point, the high-tech segment (eg mobile phones, social networks, etc.) also plays a similar role.

Investing in the stock market can be a business that can increase its capital. In addition to technical knowledge, we need some moral skills: patience, perseverance, lucidity, foresight. All qualities that must be cultivated and that can make the difference. Vice versa will never give good fruits an approach based on imprudence, on haste, from the frenzy of profit.

9. Use the leverage

What unfortunately many traders do not consider is investing in the stock market or trading online using leverage. To invest in the stock market with little money, it is necessary to deepen the study of this tool, which will allow us to expose our capital to a huge risk. We recommend the use of leverage only on a reduced capital, carried out concurrently also with a rationalized use of stop loss and take profit. In addition, you must always have your budget under control using careful Money Management. Finally, before investing in the stock market you need to study the markets and all the financial instruments on which you want to invest in.

10. You do not need to be a finance guru to invest in the stock market!

Obviously, we are not telling you that the market

should not be studied or that there must be a basis for training. Who applies himself and follows the markets, deepening the subject, will always know more than others.

So we always recommend following the training path of your broker, which will allow you not to take missteps throughout the investment process. Taking advantage of the online trading demo platforms, it is possible to simulate the investment and understand where mistakes are made and avoid them when investing with a real account.

11. Use only trusty brokers

We believe that the stock market is not a market for everyone but for a few! Above all we can not recommend the stock exchange, the investments on the stock exchange to those subjects are not inclined to study at least basic and training. In this case, it is better to let go of one's own, as it is not possible to rely only on luck.

Our advice is to stay away if you do not have and do not want to learn specific skills. If you do not have a basic education, all the savings you invest will lose them in less than a month. On the contrary, instead, we recommend investing in the stock market with online trading and regulated brokers. This is because, being regulated and being subjected to strict controls, they do not put capital at risk and also the broker will provide you with a fair and complete formation. Below you will find a complete list of regulated and authorized brokers to invest with.

12. Learn technical analysis

Technical analysis is the study of price trends with the use of graphs. The interest of a technical analyst is to look for the graphic configurations that are drawn by price movements. The market trend is evaluated to understand possible future price movements.

The pure technical analysis is not based on any fundamental of the underlying activity but applies a series of technical tools drawn on the chart, in order to allow for future courses.

On the chart, price movements are usually represented by bars or candles, allowing price analysis in a certain period of time called 'timeframe'.

On a candle, the body or the central part represents the difference between opening and closing in a given period. The shadows, ie the top and bottom segments, represent the difference between the maximum and the minimum of the period considered and the opening or closing of the candle.

We can have monthly, daily, 1 hour, 5 minutes or even shorter candles.

The different colours of the candles indicate a rise or fall in the period. Usually, a green candle represents a rise in prices, which means that the closing price of the candle is higher than the opening one, while the red candle represents a drop.

The levels of the chart where prices find an obstacle are called 'levels of support or resistance'. A 'support' is the level at which a bearish price halts its downfall and potentially 'rebounds' up again. The most significant support is repeatedly tested and becomes the level of support from a technical point of view. The 'resistance' is the opposite of the support. It is the level at which a rising price finds an obstacle to rise further and instead shows a decline. Even a resistance tested several times takes on higher strategic importance.

When prices determine an important level of support but then violate it downwards, this level of support becomes an important area of resistance. The same goes for resistance that if violated on the upside turns into a significant level of support.

There are so many indicators used by technical analysts to try and predict the next price movements. One of the most used indicators is the 'simple moving average', which is calculated on a certain amount of price data and is mobile because it moves from period to period.

Given an average of a certain time frame, the most recent data is added each time, eliminating the last data in the series from the calculation. The moving average can be used as a support or dynamic resistance. The most used periods on the daily chart for the moving average are 50, 100 and 200. If prices show an important uptrend, the moving average will be an important medium / short term support, inversely if prices show a bearish trend the average mobile will be a significant dynamic resistance.

13. Learn fundamental analysis

Unlike the previous one, it is based on the study of the company and its reference market.

In practice, it is based on balance sheet data, on management's ability and credibility, on trends in the specific sector in which the company operates. In this case, one must also consider:

5. value investing;
6. growth investing;
7. investment.

All traders have a different investing style. Every trader has his own investment techniques and each has his own particular techniques, as well as his particular tricks and his particular "secrets".

But do not be fooled by the strange idea of being able to learn how to invest by reading articles on the internet. This is impossible. You can find excellent advice but not the magic formula. At most, you could clear your mind and give yourself a general orientation, but to get serious you need longer and more in-depth things.

14. Analyse the state of the market

Closely connected to the concept of technical analysis and fundamental analysis is the concept of analysis of the general market. It does not matter whether you are a professional investor or a beginner, this will be the most difficult step you need to understand.

In practice, it is pure art applied to scientific instruments. You must first understand and analyse the market for the sole purpose of formulating a plausible development scenario. This also means accumulating an enormous amount of data and statistics regarding the performance of the securities and developing the "sensitivity" necessary to choose the truly relevant ones.

If you put this into practice you will also understand why many investors buy the shares of a particular company and not of another one.

At the same time, we always advise you to observe the products you have at home. Although this element may seem unusual, it is very important to understand that you have direct knowledge of many products and not others. In practice it will allow you to perform a quick and intuitive analysis of the financial performance of the manufacturing companies, comparing them with those of their competitors...

Before investing you must reflect on the products examined; For example, try to imagine the economic conditions for which you might decide to stop buying them or increase or decrease your stocks. This is a great exercise to get a feeling of what an average person needs and treats as "important".

15. Create an investment plan

A very important step. You have to create an investment plan, but to do that you must first of all fully understand why you want to invest.

You must know how much you can invest in and how much you want to invest in achieving your goals. You must also have clear ideas about what your goals are.

To do this you could always use an Excel sheet or even a special tool to calculate how much you will have to spend to achieve your goals.

Based on the income you can afford to invest then, calculate the type of investment. You can not claim to want to get € 10,000 from an investment if what you can afford to invest in trading online or on the stock exchange or even in other systems does not exceed 1000 euros. Everything must be proportionate. Start small and build it up over time.

16. Understand Asset Location

Defined as the distribution of liquidity in the various investment instruments available should vary depending on the stage of life in which you are.

This means that if you are young, the percentage of your investment portfolio relative to the shares will have to be higher. On the contrary, if you have a solid and well paid career, your job is like an obligation! You can use it in order to guarantee long-term income.

Here's all this allows you to allocate most of your financial portfolio in shares.

At the same time you have to understand that if you have a job whose remuneration is not predictable, as in the case where you are self employed, then you have to allocate most of your financial portfolio in more stable products; in this case, it is better to invest in bonds, perhaps government bonds and not in shares.

At the same time, however, you must consider that the actions allow faster growth of your invested assets but as such entails greater risk.

17. Study the financial risk

Another element to take into consideration when choosing to invest in a stock exchange is a financial risk. We could define it as the risk linked to the fact that investment can go wrong.

This also assumes that the yield is lower than expected or may even go red.

So be careful not to underestimate this element. On the other hand, it is an element that is not easy to understand and accept. At the same time, it is not infrequent and it is due to different dimensions that it is always good to know.

The financial risk has, in fact, different facets. In practice it could be of a different nature:

6. Specific: linked to the performance of the single instrument we purchased;
7. Systematic: linked to the oscillation of the financial market of the manager: linked to the skills of those who manage yours;
8. Money related: be it an investment fund manager, or a financial planner or consultant to whom you have been entrusted;
9. Market timing: the possibility of making mistakes when entering and/or leaving the market;
10. Liquidity: the possibility of having to sell a stock that has a little market (it is called a little liquid title) and to have a low price;
11. Currency: when buying a security denominated in foreign currency, the yield will also depend on the ratio between the currency and the euro.

Analysed according to these elements, financial risk is a bit more complex than the simple possibility that things go wrong. Understanding it and knowing how to manage these different risks can, therefore, shift the odds that things are going well in our favour.

18. Analyse and discover your risk tolerance

Another important element even before starting to invest in the stock market is to analyse one's risk appetite.

All financial instruments are characterized by a different risk. For example, the price of a stock varies over time more than that of a bond.

Unfortunately, this should not be considered a reductive element. The risk is much higher than it might seem at first.

In fact, analysing a long-term time horizon and considering an investment in US stocks that have historically made very good and therefore considering them as a safe investment, we must always consider the risk that we could incur the complete loss of the capital invested for a joke of the market that you did not foresee. So you must also consider these factors.

Here it is better to consider and analyse a more ambitious investment look. This means considering the investment portfolio and not a single instrument.

To date there are different ways to make different instruments coexist; some of these are also quite risky; on the contrary, there are others that can be considered less risky and as such reduce the overall risk of the investment.

19. Improve your Financial Intelligence

You are not born as a trader but you can become one. Investors are not born like that but they become one. How? By studying and applying. Here, in this case, brokers offer you the right solution to your problem, professional training courses also thanks to free video lessons such as those offered by the IQ Option broker dedicated entirely to the financial markets and online trading.

Financial competence takes into consideration two very important aspects: competence and time. These are very important elements that can really change the cards on the table, and make a style of investment manageable and profitable that instead for others could become an anxiety-generating bloodbath.

Regarding the risk and its propensity to face it, the questions to be asked are 2.

2. The first is inherent in the time you have

available to learn and therefore how much energy you are willing to devote to your investments.

3. The second is how anxious you are about money and economic security. In this case, it is better to let go of this whole investing idea.

20. Buy stocks of a company without competitors

Even this advice may seem improper, but in reality it is very effective.

For example, it is never advisable to invest in retail and automotive airlines, generally they are not considered good long-term investments.

In most cases these are commercial sectors in which competition is very high. This means that if you look at their balance sheets, you can see how the profits are very low.

In general, do not invest in companies that generate a large part of their turnover in specific periods of the year, as are the airlines and those related to retail sales. Only in the case in which instead they have not shown profits and constant revenues even in a long period of time, then it is convenient to do so.

21. Keep yourself updated about the news in the market

Always try to find all possible information before buying any shares. Choose only companies that have a certain solidity. Choose those that have a price momentarily lower than their real value. This concept is the essence behind the investments. You buy low and sell high.

We consider it as the keystone of being disciplined in carrying out the researches and the related market analyses and in evaluating the performance of an investment by constantly checking it and making the necessary changes.

An example would be companies with an excellent brand, which can be a good investment option.

Coca-Cola, Johnson & Johnson, Procter & Gamble, 3M and Exxon are all good examples.

22. Do not look at your portfolio every hour

This is because markets are volatile; so you do not have to be influenced by the performance of world stock exchanges, because otherwise you may even be tempted to liquidate your positions too early, losing an excellent long-term investment opportunity.

You must also consider before buying the shares of a stock, questions such as: If the value of my shares were to go down, would I be more inclined to liquidate or buy more?

If you decide to liquidate them, do not buy any other shares.

23. Be aware of your prejudices and do not allow the emotions to influence your decisions

You must always believe in what you do and never get overwhelmed by emotion. Always believe in yourself and in the strategy behind your investments. Only in this way, you will be on your way to becoming a successful investor.

All stock exchanges, like Wall Street, are focused on short-term investments.

This is why it is difficult to predict possible future profits, in case they are projected in the long term.

In order to calculate the target of your investment (the price at which to sell your positions), make forecasts with a time horizon of more than 10 years and update them over time using the DCF.

24. Invest in those companies that hold shareholders in high esteem

In most cases, companies prefer to spend profits on buying a new personal jet for the CEO instead of paying dividends to shareholders.

A long-term management-oriented remuneration system, "stock-expensing", even if it is a prudent capital investment policy, a reliable dividend policy, a profit for growth stocks and the BVPS ("Book-Value-Per- Share ") are all indicators of a company oriented towards its shareholders.

25. Try out "paper trading"

In this case, it is a simulation of investments. In practice, this tool keeps track of the price of the shares and of all of your purchase and sale transactions, as if you were actually operating them on the market.

At the same time, you can check your investments if they have generated a profit or not.

Once you have identified a reliable and profitable strategy and you feel comfortable with the natural functioning of the market, you can move on to the real operational phase.

Finally, remember that you are not buying and selling

worthless pieces of paper; the price rises and falls over time; you are buying shares in real companies.

Your decision to buy the shares of a particular company should be influenced only by two factors: the economic soundness of the company and the price of its shares.

26. Focus your thoughts

When analyzing the market, you should always try to formulate a plausible development scenario and consequently identify the good securities to invest in. We are sure that this passage serves you in order to make some forecasts on some specific areas.

An example would be the trend in interest rates and inflation, if not the way in which these variables can affect the yield of fixed-rate financial products or other assets. At the same time, when interest rates are low, it could be expected that consumers and businesses can access cash and credit more easily.

In practice, all this means that people have more money to use for their purchases and therefore tend to buy more.

At the same time, companies, thanks to higher revenues, will be able to invest with the aim of expanding their activities.

On the contrary, the opposite happens in the stock market; low interest rates lead to an increase in the price of equities. At the same time, a high interest rate generates a lowering of the value of the shares.

At a time when interest rates are high, investing becomes much more expensive. So you could try to invest in shares that offer a better return for you but that are not heavy for consumers.

An example could be the bank's shares. If you invest on the shares of a Bank X because the interest rates are high for you, you must also consider the interest rates that are applied to those who ask for a mortgage, for example. In this case, an interest rate for a high mute will soon make Bank shares collapse because it is not convenient for the lender. Always evaluate all factors then.

In short, consumers spend less and companies have less liquidity for investments and therefore there is a slowdown in economic growth or even a stalemate.

27. Create a wish list

In order to be able to establish your financial goals, you must always have a precise idea of the things or experiences you wish to possess. You can always choose only what you want to experience in life, and for which you need to earn money.

You must have a list of everything you want to get from this investment and then work out a lineup to guarantee your goals.

28. Diversify your portfolio

Investors with an experience like Warren Buffett recommend diversifying their investments. A choice that serves to manage risks in a better way, as do the most prudent that focus on companies in different industries and in different countries, hoping that a bad event does not damage all their titles: "Imagine owning five different companies. At the end of the year, the company A and B performed well and increased the value of the shares by 25%. C and D instead increased by 10%. While E was the most unlucky and ended up in liquidation. In this case, the diversification strategy helps you recover the losses of your total investment.

29. Understand the main financial instruments

Among the many solutions that are available to those who intend to invest, we want to talk about: Forex, binary options, ETFs and commodities.

Proceeding by order, we clarify how Forex investments work. It is the largest market in the world today. Although it is simple to deposit and therefore invest in the ratio of currencies, it is certainly known that returns are so high as the same measure of losses. It is for this reason that experts are always advised to take advantage of the demos for general learning before proceeding with the use of real money. In any case, it is our advice to beginners to focus only on the performance of a currency pair, remembering to include the stop loss in the open position to avoid too large losses.

In regard to investments in binary options, these are available to anyone, like the previous solution, provided that some attention is always paid in these circumstances. This investment system concerns the launch of forecasts aimed at the performance of a certain security over a given period of time. To be expected, there is if the course will be positive or negative in times defined by the trader who can go from a minimum of 60 seconds up to months. If the forecast is correct, there will be rather interesting profits. Even here, in order not to face unpleasant surprises, the same goes for the previous type of investment.

The ETF, those funds listed in real time that we mentioned, which go to replicate the index of a certain basket of securities, allow you to invest even with small amounts at lower costs than traditional funds. With these, you can trade on a wide variety of indices such as emerging markets, entire geographical areas, individual states, listed companies and more. The advantages of investing using ETFs reside not only in their convenience, in being very liquid and tradable like equities, but also in the respective assets independent of the issuer.

30. Consider it a serious business

I truly believe that anyone can learn to trade options, currencies (Forex), commodities (Commodities) or cryptocurrencies. In the same way, I am convinced that with this system you can become financially free. But it must be approached as a serious business.

Let me ask you a question: how much did you study or work to achieve the experience you have in your current job? I imagine we are talking about several years and still thousands of hours of study and practice.

Trading is not different. When trading, you compete on a par with people who do it by profession: you must, therefore, have humility, work, perseverance, intelligence, and method. If you really apply, in a few months you can decide to give up your job because you can earn a lot of money with something that requires commitment and constancy, but without being stressed or having to spend all day on the trading sites. Never stop studying, learning and improving: it's what most people need.

Chapter 8

Not only real estate

Another great way to invest your money is to invest it in a business. Here are some ways you can do that.

Let's see what the main ways to create a passive and automatic monthly online income are:

4. Sell one or more services, automating the process as much as possible.
5. Sell content, in the form of books, ebooks, courses or info-products.
6. Selling through others, earning from affiliation.
7. Monetize content published in other ways (eg with advertising space)

At the moment I (like many others here in America and in the rest of the world) earn from all 4 sources.

Naturally, each of these ways of creating passive income presupposes the initial work and, in many cases, also the subsequent work although sporadic to maintain the vitality of the source of income. As you have noticed, in fact, in all three cases we talk about "selling", which presupposes that there are buyers and that there is a need to reach them by letting them know in some way (possibly without investing in advertising), and at the same time that there is a "product" to sell to these people, something that may interest them for any reason.

We will try to examine this four ways one by one so that you can understand which one is the best one for you, that is, with which you feel more affinity in relation to your interests, your passions, and your abilities.

1. Passive income from the sale of services or online applications

This is one of the most effective methods to create an automated passive online income, but unlike the other three methods presented below it requires a small investment to register a suitable domain and Web space, as well as greater technical expertise.

For this type of passive income, in fact, we consider services such as ad sites or those that allow you to manage technical aspects of activity on the Web, proposed in the freemium formula, or with a free basic version that involves limitations of use and a more complete paid version where the limitations are 'unlocked'.

In the first category there are, for example, sites where people can post ads of various kinds made with themes or dedicated plugins (using CMS as WordPress), such as those for the sale of used equipment or to meet other people (ad sites) or online dating, or tourist portals that give visibility to advertisers and earn every time they sell their service (it is the case of the hospitality industry with sites like TripAdvisor, Wimdu, etc.), or other sites that put freelancers with potential customers in connection, and so on.

In the second category, on the other hand, there may be included sites that manage, for example, the backup of a site or its maintenance, facilitate networking or collaborative activities of a professional nature, and so on. It goes without saying that it is not enough to develop and put online this type of services, but that we must then promote them both initially and periodically so that more and more people are registered, and naturally we must manage them with an equally regular maintenance to avoid problems of stability or security on the site that provides them.

In addition to the sites, there may also be true applications, both in the form of computer software (desktop PC) and mobile devices (smartphones and tablets) in the form of an app. In this case, the skills required for their development are even greater, and once again there will be a need for promotion to make them known and updated over time to correct any stability and security bugs or improve their functionality making them even more attractive. Of this second sector are, of course, also the games, often proposed with a freemium formula and distributed as an app or inserted into websites (eg in gambling or multi-user games) or on social networks. Probably those who read will have already had the opportunity to play some of these games, or to take advantage of some services like those listed above.

At this point, it will be clearer what we mean when we say that there is no totally passive income, a concept that we will find even later, and it is, therefore, important to underline.

2. Passive income from the sale of contents

When we talk about content we refer not only to those that form an ebook or a book, but also to images that a photographer can sell on sites specialized in stock images, or to video and to the audio sold in the same way. In all these cases, passive income streams will derive from the repeated sale of each individual content, which may produce a proper revenue if it is conducted on its own or partial if sold through a distribution platform. The latter are represented, for example, by traditional book stores or those online in the case of books and ebooks, from the already mentioned sites that sell images (photos and drawings), video or audio for professional purposes such as the development of sites or multimedia products, or again from sites that host, for example, online courses if the contents already mentioned represent, for example, a video course or an audio course.

In all these cases, the content must be produced only once and then placed on the market through an automated sales system, and this is how the flow of passive income is created resulting from its sale. As can be understood, even for content, promotion and marketing are essential if we want to increase sales rather than simply wait for someone to notice them and buy them (something that happens), and for those contents that are subject to obsolescence (for, for example, courses on technical subjects) it is also necessary to proceed with periodic updates so that they remain attractive to the public and do not become too old (and therefore no longer valid) because someone decides to buy them again.

A strategy often used by those who live from the production of content is to offer a part (or a 'fragmented' version) for free, for example through a site or a blog, and create parallel commercial versions that collect them as a book/ebook, full course, and so on. In this way it becomes possible to create a 'showcase' able to support the commercially distributed 'works', and thus increase sales.

3. Passive income from affiliate marketing

If you do not want to sell your services, products or content, you can always do it with those of others by earning a percentage of those sales and thus creating another form of passive income. In this case, however, the sale takes place outside of your site, directly on that of the seller. In America, the opportunities for affiliation are many and offer ample earning space.

Passive affiliate streams of income can also derive from sources other than a website, for example from content published on social networks, but in this case they have a shorter duration in time as they go into the background as time passes and it becomes less likely that the public will notice them and click on the respective links (unless you periodically invest in paid visibility, as you do for example on Facebook, highlighting the payment of a post, but in this case we will fall into passive generated by a cash investment, however minimal, so it is not appropriate to include it in this chapter. Do not worry, we will talk about passive streams of income that require a money investment in the next chapter.

4. Passive returns from other monetization of contents

The latter category may include, for example, services such as the sale, or rather the rental of advertising space on a site or app that enjoys a certain popularity/visibility. The advertising spaces can be represented by the text in a directory, by banners or entire pages, as happens for example in the sites/portals that are positioned in the tourism sector and rent a space to managers of the hotel, restaurant, and similar activities inside of strategic areas of the site. What has just been said at the end of the previous paragraph is more valid than ever in such a field, given that advertisers will be more likely to pay their periodic share the more they are certain of gaining visibility through the site.

The same applies to the app, once they have achieved the necessary popularity, but the latter typically requires investments in marketing and advertising to gain visibility among the public.

To have life insurance you must be healthy (and what you pay each year varies from many factors. You must never omit anything about your state of health to the insurance company as it may not pay coverage to the beneficiaries in case of premorence of the insured! In addition, insurance companies often recommend splitting insurance into two that should last 20 years (your child is 5 years old and you want to cover it from the risk of loss of income until the hypothetical end of the university study path). This is explained to you as an advantage in financial terms. The advantage is actually there because you save some money. But you must dwell on the final purpose of TCM. In your opinion, is it to gain or protect those dear to you from your lack? Exactly the second answer is the right one! So returning to the example what would happen if your health conditions worsen when your first 10-year insurance expires and the insurance company does not make you a new TCM for the next 10 years? Nothing at all! You have to cross your fingers and hope to have accumulated enough to make your child survive better, hoping to be able to enroll him at the university! So forget if you want to make money with TCM. By their nature they only serve to protect your loved ones and to get rid of the most feared question: and if I will not be there next year, who will take care of my family?

So the TCM, like many other types of insurance (there are 24 insurance branches provided for by the Insurance Code), are used to avoid unpleasant surprises in the future. These risks, of course, are unpredictable and I do not expect them to happen to anyone, and we should not try to predict them when they happen. We need only to build protection through insurance policies. To confirm this, I quote the quote from world-renowned investor Warren Buffet: "it is not necessary to predict the rain, but it is important to know how to build the Ark"

The best way to destroy debt forever is not to start paying it immediately but to create a business that gives you cash flow that you can use to pay off the debt. Here are some creative ways to do it.

Flipping online businesses

Flippa is the number one portal for selling and buying websites: it boasts a huge audience and offers excellent tools to increase the visibility of your online auction. If you are going to commit a bit of capital, a little time and a lot of "rags", the buying and selling of sites on Flippa could bring you great profits and build, over time, a nice income stream.

The platform has sold sites for 140 million dollars since the launch in 2009. If you want to contribute to increasing this amount, you should read the following pages.

Find a niche

Before investing a single euro or dollar, you must be clear about what your site will look like and what it will talk about. In this phase, it is good to find a niche with potential and start from that. Alternatively, if you think you have knowledge on a certain topic that can be considered a niche, then desing the blog in that direction.

Focusing on a specific "small" sector is already a first step in cutting out large numbers of competitors. Obviously, the niche must have at least a little bit of a client base, you do not want to work for nothing, right?

Building Vs. Buying

Well, you found your industry, now it's about securing a site and then the doubt that arises is built it or buy it? Let's see what are the pros and cons of both cases.

1. Build your site

Unless you're a web developer, creating a site from scratch can cost you a few hundred dollars - unless you buy one already existing, anyway. You can also follow an ad hoc course, but the quickest way is definitely to hire a programmer who does the "dirty work" and build your blog on a solid foundation.

It would be good to create it on WordPress. Those who buy websites, generally, know this platform and therefore tend to buy preferably WordPress sites. Once the site is set up, you need content that is focused on keywords and full of affiliate links.

The ways to follow are essentially two: either you create all the content or pay someone to do it for you. Sites like Fiverr put you in touch with copywriters, writers, graphic designers and much more (the texts cost an average of $5 for 500 words).

When you have accumulated a lot of material, avoid publishing it all in one step and dilute it over time, following the classical one/two articles per day patter.

2. Buy your site

Very often buying a site already started will cost you more than creating it from scratch, but at the same time, you will enjoy some significant benefits. First of all, a consolidated public (more or less numerous), and according to the site will already be indexed on search engines.

The key point is to buy it for less than it actually is worth. You must be careful of at least three factors when approaching a seller of underserved sites:

3. the owner does not update it very often;
4. the site does not make much money;
5. the owner seems disinterested in his business

If you find something with these features, consider making an offer. But if finding the "perfect site" that meets these requirements becomes too exhausting or steals too much time, you can rely on a site broker. Many of these are commissioned and have access to huge databases of sites. Just tell them the key points and they will find the site that's right for you.

Once you have purchased the site, use all the means you have to grow it, increase traffic and earn money.

Sell sites on Flippa

When your site has achieved good traffic, engagement and the financial potential it is time to put it on auction on Flippa. Here are some suggestions for creating a successful auction.

1. Prepare a detailed description

As also reported by Flippa in a blog post, the auctions that are less successful are those with little information in the descriptions. Few data available reflect the shortage of the seller and the site itself. Possible buyers might think that if you did not want to write a description, how distract can you have managed your site?

Try to write an understandable text, with a professional tone, able to generate interest and inspire security.

2. Enter the statistics

It may seem obvious, but the first thing that a possible

buyer will read will be the statistics of your site. So make sure that they are as up-to-date as possible, especially with regard to page views and gross revenue.

3. Do not be anonymous

Try to imagine to place hundreds of dollars of an offer to a seller without a name, without a face or without a social account, would you rather not know who you are dealing with? Those who buy feel much safer to negotiate with a real person, especially when the price of the site begins to be important. Your name, your face tells the buyer that you have nothing to hide and you are not a scam artist. The first thing you need to earn is your client's trust, the second is his money.

4. Reach the "most active categories" on Flippa

If your auction is very popular, Flippa could put it in the "most active" category. This does not cost you anything, but it gives you a lot of visibility, putting you in front of thousands of buyers. The advice I've given you so far should help you get more offers, but if you realize they are less than you expect, try the following.

Let's say you've launched an auction and you already received an offer in the early hours, as a seller you can decide whether to accept it or wait to receive more. Once you approve the first, the others will follow automatically. If you set aside more offers without approving them and then do it at once, Flippa's algorithm acknowledges that your auction is very busy. So you have more chances to finish among the "Most Active" ones.

5. Create a sustainable product

How much maintenance does your site require? How much will the buyer have to work to make it profitable? Offers may stop if buyers realize that the site needs more time than it actually is worth.

So try not to worry about them and make sure your site is sustainable. Starting from the contents. Let's say that they are all flour of your lot and that has allowed you to save money. But think how the customer can react knowing that he will have to look for and hire a freelance to create new posts.

If you have been relying on external writers right from the start, just pass them on to the new owner who will then have to deal with experienced collaborators.

6. Reach all potential buyers

Do not rely on the only offers you receive, try to be active in the search for new buyers as well. If the promotion through social media is not enough, contact directly the owners of the sites that are part of your niche. Maybe they may be interested in buying your site to increase earnings, or just to permanently eliminate competition.

Buying and selling sites on Flippa is not an activity you can do in one night, but if you invest time and energy you can get excellent profits. Remember to buy or create a site that belongs to a profitable niche and make it grow so that it generates money. When you place the auction on Flippa make sure you take advantage of all the promotion channels and always be transparent with your potential customers.

I have always liked this business model because it allows anyone to start their little empire with little money. 100$ are often enough to create a powerful website that will attract buyers on Flippa. After you have made your first profit, it is important to use it to fuel the business and create another website to sell.

Sooner than later, you will have enough capital to outsource the creation of the sites and you will find yourself collecting money on autopilot. How can you do it? I highly recommend visiting Upwork.com, a powerful website that allows you to find hundreds, if not thousands, of virtual assistants that can be hired for cheap (most of them work for 2-3$ per hour) and instruct them to post your listings on Flippa. I have done this before and I really loved the freedom that outsourcing the listing part gave me. My favourite VA and the one I collaborate with to this day is Ammar Shafiq: I highly recommend him to you.

If you do not want to go down the Upwork route, you can always try to find virtual assistants of Facebook groups or on other platforms. Just keep in mind that when you are not using a centralized and controlled platform, you are more likely to bump into scammers and people that do not take things as seriously as they should.

Dropship your way out of debt

We have come to one of my favourite online business models. Dropshipping is a retail model where the store does not hold stock of products but only buys them after the purchase from the client has already happened.

The supplier - typically a wholesaler or a manufacturer - receives the order and takes care of the shipment to the final customer, without specifying his identity. The result is that, in the eyes of the customer, the entire transaction is managed by the store that does not actually even see the product that is sold.

To better understand how it works, let's take a concrete example.

Suppose that amazinglamps.com is an online store specializing in - guess what - lamps, which operates using dropshipping with a wholesaler in the sector. When Mr.Brown decides to buy a lamp for his daughter's wedding, does a search on Google and finds a perfect lamp for her house.

This is exactly what happens, step by step.

Step 1 - Mr.Brown places an order on amazinglamps.com

Once he chose his lamp, Mr.Brown completes the purchase by making a payment of $80 with a credit card and indicating his shipping address. The payment is deposited in the account of amazinglamps.com and Mr.Brown receives an automatic confirmation email.

Step 2 - amazinglamps.com passes the order to its supplier

Together with the confirmation email addressed to Mr.Brown, the e-commerce platform of amazinglamps.com automatically sends an email to the supplier with all the order details including the item code ordered and the shipping address. Amazinglamps.com has already left a credit card to its supplier to use for each order. The supplier, therefore, uses this card by withdrawing an amount of $50, or the cost of the lamp according to the price list reserved for amazinglamps.com.

Step 3 - The supplier sends the lamp to Mr.Brown

The supplier sends the ordered article to Mr.Brown, using a package with the amazinglamps.com logo. Once the order has been sent, the supplier sends a confirmation email to amazinglamps.com, including the $50 invoice and the tracking number for tracking the shipment on the shipper's website.

Step 4 - amazinglamps.com warns Mr.Brown of the shipment

Once the shipping confirmation has been received from the supplier, the manager of amazinglamps.com uses its e-commerce platform to send a confirmation email to Mr.Brown.

The email also contains the tracking number and a link to the shipper's website that Mr.Brown can use to track the position of his package in real time.

Step 5, the big step - Mr.Brown receives his lamp and happily gifts it to his daughter

After a couple of days, Mr.Brown receives the package of amazinglamps.com and shows satisfied his purchase to his wife, who finds the lamp very elegant. The following week, Mr.Brown gifts the lamp to his daughter.

Despite its fundamental role, throughout the transaction, the supplier is completely invisible to

Mr.Brown. On the package, there is the logo of amazinglamps.com and there is never any reference to those involved in packaging and shipping the package.

In fact, the wholesaler is as if it did not exist for the final customer. His sole responsibility is to store the products and send them when an order is received. Everything else - development and management of the e-commerce site, marketing activities, customer service, etc. - is the responsibility of the retailer.

This model is often referred to as the ultimate solution for those who want to start an online business. Without a doubt, it is the simplest model but in fact, has its pros and cons that I want to show you one by one.

Benefits

Minimum investment - Probably the biggest advantage of dropshipping is the possibility of launching an e-commerce store without having to invest thousands of dollars for the purchase of products. With the dropshipping model, in fact, you do not have to buy any product until the moment you have already sold it and you have already received payment from your customer. It is, therefore, possible to start a successful dropshipping business with an investment close to zero.

Easy to get started - Carrying out an e-commerce business is much easier when you are not dealing with physical products. With dropshipping you do not have to worry about:

4. Managing or pay for a warehouse;
5. Packing and shipping your orders;
6. Keeping track of inventory;
7. Managing returns;
8. Managing stock reorders.

Reduced expenses - Not having to deal with the advance purchase of products in the catalogue or with the management of the warehouse, your expenses are very low. You can safely run a dropshipping business from home with your laptop, spending less than $50 a month for your Shopify store plus some useful accounting tool.

As your business grows, your expenses also increase, but they will always be very low compared to those who run traditional e-commerce or even a physical store.

Independence from the workplace - A dropshipping business can be managed from anywhere in the world as long as there is an Internet connection. All you need to do is update your site, communicate with customers and pass orders by email to suppliers. If you think about it, this aspect is very important and can literally change your life.
You will probably never work lying in a hammock on a tropical island but the fact that you can do it will make you feel better. If nothing else, you can choose your usual place of work, away from the chaos and traffic and this will make your routine much better.

Wide range of products - Not having to buy the products you sell in advance, means that you can add to your catalogue all the products that suppliers provide you with. If a product is in stock, you can sell it on your e-commerce site at no additional cost. Despite this is a great advantage, you have to be careful not to get too caught up, putting up an online super store that sells everything. Most people prefer niche stores rather than larger ones.

Even with dropshopping, it is essential to select a specific niche that gives your business a clear and well-defined shape.

Scalability - With a traditional business, if you receive double orders you typically have to work twice as hard to sort them out. With dropshipping, however, most of the work is done by your suppliers allowing you to grow without weighing on your shoulders too much. Especially if your processes are automated, you will actually have an increase in work only for customer service.

On Shopify there is a very popular app that allows you to put the autopilot to your online store, taking care of sorting the orders in real time to one or more of your suppliers based on the products sold.

All these benefits make dropshipping a very attractive model for both beginners and experienced traders. Unfortunately, they are not all sunshine and rainbows.

All this convenience and flexibility has a price to pay.

Disadvantages

Low margins - The main problem with dropshipping is the low margins per order that can usually be obtained. This is because buying a product only after selling it, you can not use the same price lists that are reserved for those who buy large volumes in advance. As a result, to remain competitive and not go off-market with the selling price, you have no choice but to keep your top ups low.

As we have seen, the perfect product to sell online has a surcharge of 500% compared to the purchase price. With dropshipping, you can forget about a margin of this kind and you can expect to reach 30-40% at the most.

To mitigate this problem, you can always deal with your suppliers when your sales become regular and your orders, even if diluted over time, start to have important numbers. However, this will not happen in the first few months of your business, so you'll have to consider fairly tight initial earnings.

Problems with products availability - If you manage your products, it is relatively easy to track the availability of what you are selling. If on the contrary, you supply from one or more wholesalers who distribute your products to other merchants, the availability can vary very quickly within a day.

In theory, you could solve this problem by integrating with your suppliers' warehouse software, but this is not always a viable path, also because the technological equipment of your suppliers may not be as evolved as you would like.

Complex shipping costs - If you work with more than one supplier, you may have products in the same order that will be shipped from different warehouses, multiplying shipping costs.

For example, if your customer enters an order with two products belonging to two different wholesalers, two parcels must be shipped and shipping costs will be double. To offer a quality service, you will have to pay for these additional expenses resulting in a loss on your profit margin.

Vendor errors - Have you ever been accused of

something that you did not have any fault but that fell under your responsibility?

Even the best suppliers make mistakes and when it happens you'll have to take on all the responsibilities and apologize to your customer. Remember that in his eyes there is only your store and as well as giving you positive feedback in the case of a good shopping experience, he will complain to you in case of problems with his order.

As Grant Cardone said, "you don't want to get rich fast, you want to get rich for sure". When you are starting out, it is easy to get caught up in get rich quick schemes. However, the best way is to invest early in emerging markets and enjoy the profits in the long run. An example? Cryptocurrencies and blockchain projects.

The issue with cryptocurrencies is that being a market that is not yet regulated in several countries, the risk of pumps and dumps, manipulation and fraud is just around the corner. This is why I wanted to cover them in this book. In fact, since they provide a great opportunity, I am worried that a lot of people may get involved without knowing what they are doing and will lose a lot of money down the line. Here I want to show you what I do before investing in a particular asset and how I keep it a sustainable source of passive income.

Before getting started, here is a list of useful tools for the analysis of cryptocurrencies:

- Coincheckup.com - one of my favourite sites, offers much more data than other cryptocurrency monitoring sites;
- Coinmarketcap.com - one of the oldest crypto price tracking sites, far more popular than Coincheckup, but offers less data;
- Blockfolio - another popular cryptocurrency tracker.

Now let's get to the good stuff.

Step 1 - Understanding your risk profile

Many people will advise you to buy "low capitalization" cryptocurrencies and tokens (ie between 10 and 100 million dollars) because they have a greater opportunity for growth in terms of percentage.

Although this statement is relatively correct, you have to keep in mind that the smaller a coin is, the riskier it is to invest in it. Why? Because the project has indeed a much higher risk of failing.

In traditional investments, most people aim and are happy to get an annual return of 3% - 4%; but they could be in serious financial difficulty if the invested capital is lost, so most of the time more well-known, safer and more stable titles are selected.
Other people would instead be satisfied only with an annual yield of 7% - 12%. These people could also be willing to lose all their investment if things go wrong. In their case, they would point to a higher risk given the economic attitude they have at the base.

These two different groups of people have different "risk profiles".

It is important that in any purchase you make in your life (even for something "concrete" like a car), you do so knowingly about the financial risk profile you can afford to take.
My personal opinion is that just because something

has higher chances of performance does not mean it is the best choice. In particular, I have invested mainly in the top 5 coins in terms of capitalization, because they are the safest spot right now. However, I always allocate a small part of my portfolio, 10% to be precise, to low cap coins. How do I find the most promising one? Here is what I do.

Step 2 - Identification of new coins or tokens

There are three main ways I usually use to find the "new" coins or tokens:

8. Through the posts of the Bitcointalk.org forum, more precisely in the section "Announcements (Altcoins)";
9. In the subreddit / r / cryptocurrency;
10. In the "Newly Added" sections of Coincheckup and "Recently Added" by Coinmarketcap.

Each of these is a great resource to discover interesting coins with great return potential over a shorter period of time. As already said, I only put in at maximum 10% of my capital into these underrated projects.

With every investment comes the possibility to get scammed and in the crypto world happens more often that I would like to see. During the last three years of experience, I have developed a series of principles that I follow in order to avoid being scammed. Here is what will make me decide NOT to invest in an asset.

Step 3 - Exclusion of coins and useless tokens/scams

One of the first things I do when I look at new projects is to subject them to very strict criteria to remove "fluf" projects from the list. In particular:

7. I do not buy cryptocurrencies in industries and sectors that I do not understand;
8. I do not buy cryptocurrencies whose teams are inactive in social media communication;
9. I do not buy cryptocurrencies whose startups/associations/companies are registered in countries where I can not validate a solid corporate entity;
10. I do not buy cryptocurrencies if I cannot find the team members (with particular attention to the founder) on LinkedIn and validate that they

are real profiles;

11. I do not buy cryptocurrencies whose teams adopt spamming strategies and do aggressive and non informative marketing campaigns on social and non-social channels;

12. If a team is building a brand new technology, I do not buy the cryptocurrency/token unless there is a detailed technical document explaining how it works;

13. If a cryptocurrency has a pre-ICO with a discount, I tend not to buy it. If I did, it would only be in the case where the discount compared to the public ICO is minimal and the amount purchased is "locked" for a significant period of time (to avoid massive dumps after the public ICO);

14. I do not buy cryptocurrencies if I do not use them personally as an end user.

To help me with the process, I also use a series of questions that allow me to get more in depth and realize the true fundamental value of an asset. In particular, I really like to ask myself the following questions:

- Would I use this cryptocurrency as an end user?

- Would I pay that price as a user?

- Does this project require the development of new technology?

- What is the team's experience in this determined direction? Have they already managed a successful company? What was the performance of this company?

- Does the team have the ability to develop this technology? Are engineers and developers recognized in this sector? Do they have product managers and customer support?

- Is it clear how the project will generate users/customers?

- Why are they using the blockchain? Do they really need it or do they use the term "blockchain" to hype their project up? What are the pros and cons of using the blockchain in this case and why should the blockchain improve the current alternative on the market? (Keep in mind that currently, in most cases, blockchain-based systems are slow and expensive).

Pay attention to absolutist statements. Each project has negative aspects and consequences, a real project will be realistic in delineating them, especially the latter.

If I can see that each question has a positive answer, I will than allocate a part of my portfolio. I always invest long term and I am willing to stay in a coin for at least one year. If, for any reason, I do not feel confident enough to put money into a project for at least 52 weeks than that means that it is probably better to look at another one.

Predicting the next currency that will make the boom is impossible, out there are so many projects based on nothing that still capitalize tens of billions of dollars; in the same way, there are dozens of serious projects that deserve more, but that fails to stand out and gain visibility compared to others. The golden rule is that which applies in every financial market: diversify. By diversifying between several coins, you reduce the risk.

My final tip on cryptocurrency investing is to always include Bitcoin, Litecoin, Ethereum and Bitcoin Cash in your portfolio, since those are the most supported coins by institutional investors. How do I buy those coins? Everything starts on Coinbase.

An important leverage

If you want to retire early, the best way is to start using the power of compound interest. Here is what it is.

What is compound interest? Not everyone may know how to respond immediately to this question. In fact, if everyone knows what the simple interest is, ie the one that withdraws at the end of the agreed time unit, fewer are those who know what the compound interest is, how it works and, most importantly, how to take advantage of it.

The example of a bank account is enlightening.

If on 1 January I have a net rate of 1% on my account, at the end of the year I have 101 euros. The euro more is added to the capital and, if the conditions do not change, at the end of the second year I will not have 102 euros, but 102 euros and 1 cent where the cent represents 1% of the euro accumulated after the first year.

So far, everything is clear, but most of us can not calculate the compound interest of an investment and tend to treat it as simple interest. This is due to its slow start, that, especially with small capital, tend to be treated as "irrelevant". However, there is nothing more wrong that an investor could do.

If, for example, after 5 years of investment, my capital of 100 euros is now 140, we are led to believe that the interest was 8% per year.

This is incorrect because, in doing so, we do not take into account that at the end of each period the interest accumulate has gone to increase capital. If the interest had really been 8%, composing the 5 years we would have had

Initial capital: 100

- 1st year: 108
- 2nd year: 116.64
- 3rd year: 125.97
- 4th year: 136.04
- 5th year: 146.93

The difference (6.93 euros) represents almost 7% of the total. As you can see, it is easy to take dazzle (and worse, even "suffer", if for some reason we are offered a simple interest for compound interest).

The maths behind compound interest: an easy example

Suppose we have an initial capital of 1,000 euros. The capital yields a Y% interest and this interest is calculated on an annual basis.

What will be the value of the investment after X years?

The calculation formula is as follows:

(1) IV = CP (1 + Y) ^ X

IV is the value of the investment after X years, while CP is the initial capital. Y is expressed as a percentage, ie 0.04 indicates 4%. The symbol ^ is the symbol of elevation to power.

The inverse calculation tends to find the Y interest of an investment that now (net of inflation) is worth IV against a CP capital invested X periods (years) ago. The formula is:

(2) Y = (IV / CP) ^ (1 / X) - 1

Suppose that, after inflation, 1,000 euros invested 5 years ago are now worth 1,400 euros, you immediately have that the yield was 6.96%.

Let's take a look at another example
Marie has just taken the salary and can finally buy the air conditioner she needs.

But her friend Julie calls her to tell her that she has an urgent need that she can not cope with immediately and asks her to borrow € 1,000.

Marie is undecided because this would mean waiting another month before she can make her purchase.

To resolve the issue the two girls agree on the loan provided that Julie returns the money to Mary with a 5% interest (the numbers are purely random for the purposes of the example).

In this way, Marie has a greater incentive to have to delay her purchase.

When Julie returns the sum loaned, she will receive € 1,050 instead of € 1,000.

The following month Marie can then buy the air conditioner and, to celebrate, use the € 50 interest to go out to dinner with her boyfriend.

In short, in the end, this recognition for the delayed use was not bad!

Now that we understand the concept behind the rate of interest it is good to enter a little more in detail and make some distinctions.

In this regard, we can divide the interest rate into two broad categories:
15. The simple interest;
16. The compound interest.

Simple Interest

Let's go back to the previous example.

At the end of the period, Julie returns the money plus the interest to Mary. Soon after, however, the girl asks again the same amount to buy a new refrigerator, as the old one suddenly broke.

Marie agrees to lend the money back to her friend.

The following month Julie firmed up her debt plus new interests, again for a total of € 1,050.

Now Marie is with her initial capital, plus € 100 in interest, for a total of € 1,100.

Interest is defined as simple when, once it has matured on the underlying capital, it does not generate further interest.

In our example, we note that the first 50 € was not added to the capital loaned the second time.

Compound Interest

Change of scenery.

Julie asks Marie to lend her € 1,000 with the promise to return them in two years.

Mary agrees, as long as Julie accepts a compound interest on the mature borrowed capital.

In this case, Julie will not have to pay the interest

immediately at the end of the 1st year but will add the € 50 interest in the capital, which in turn will accumulate 5% in the 2nd year.

At the end of the agreed period, Julie must therefore return:

- € 1,000 capital
- € 50 interest for the first year (€ 1,000 + 5%)
- € 52.50 interest for the 2nd year (€ 1.050 + 5%)

The total capital to be returned to Mary is, therefore, € 1,102.50.

Here we have materialized € 2.50 more than the previous example, due to the compound interest.

The interest is defined as compound when, once it has matured on the underlying capital, it is added to the latter and contributes to generating further increased interest in the future.

Do you understand why the compound interest is your new best friend?

When you deposit your money in the bank account

you are doing as Marie, that is, you are "lending" your money to the bank, which uses them to perform its credit function and lend it to people and businesses.

As a reward for this service, you are given an interest in the sums deposited, that is, a reward for the fact that you delay their use.

How to take advantage of the compound interest

If you do not want inflation to eat a nice slice of the real value and the purchasing power of your money, you have to make sure that the latter accrue compound interest over time.

Certainly a part of the liquidity at your disposal you can deposit on one or more deposit accounts, or accounts with limited operations, where however higher interest rates are recognized.

For example, you could deposit your emergency fund. The rest, however, you should invest in a portfolio of efficient financial instruments that protect your capital and create added value.

The compound interest must, therefore, be exploited for at least two reasons:

- Increase savings while waiting for their use;
- Defence against inflation.

A wise thing to do is, therefore, exploit the power of compound interest to make the value of your money grow faster, protecting it from loss of purchasing power.

Try to keep only small amounts on bank accounts that give you little to nothing.

You can leave just the right liquidity for your daily expenses and for the emergency fund.

Are you looking for safe and profitable investments? Finding solutions of this type is not easy, you know very well and that's why you decided to take the smartphone, the PC or the tablet to deepen.

In this chapter, we have decided to provide you with 3 concrete solutions to invest immediately, without making endless queues in the bank and without losing control of what you do.

The strategies that we suggest are ordered according to the risk profile, so we start from the less risky ones to get to the more aggressive ones.

We have written it in several books of this series, we underline it here too for safety: there are no safe investments and at the same time with double-digit returns. The times of government bonds and generous postal coupons have long since come to a close, the current economic situation sees interest at historic lows owing to the ECB's manoeuvrers in recent years.

In summary:

Few risks = Few Earnings
Many Risks = Potentially Increased Earnings but
High Chances for Huge Losses

We come now to the merit of our discussion, here are the best solutions for investing that we have chosen for you.

1. Santander Consumer Bank is the most remunerative deposit account

Are you looking for 100% capital guarantee? The deposit account is the best solution even if, in light of the considerations made before, you do not have to expect double-digit returns.

The best deposit account of the moment is that of Santander Consumer Bank which offers you an annual 1.8% on deposits at 36 months.

The advantages of Santander's offer can be summarized as follows:

- 100% security;
- Open it online: no stress, if you are from a PC you just need to fill out a form (you can do the same thing if you are on a smartphone) and just leave a few data. The procedure will be completed by phone at the time you indicated;
- No penalty in case of early release: if you withdraw money before the scheduled time, you lose nothing;
- o Opening costs and management fees: you do not have to pay anything to make money.

To all this, we must add that Santander also provides the unconstrained option that allows you to receive 0.5% per year on free sums. This option can be mixed with the tied one: for example, out of 30 thousand euros, 20 thousand can be tied up at an interest rate of 1.8%, while the remaining 10 thousand free ones receive 0.5%.

Santander is a solid institution, active throughout the world with 122 million customers and over 160 years of history and is now the best solution for those looking for a deposit account free of risks and concerns.

2. MoneyFarm: the tech alternative to deposit accounts

Moneyfarm is an Italian startup that has created a convenient platform to invest online: it is easy to understand and it is safe, we have also explained it in our review.

You can earn up to 5.41%.
The bank deposit accounts, at this stage, have returns that only in a few cases exceed 1.5%. If you're looking

for granitic safety, go back to paragraph 1 where we talk about Santander.

However, if you are looking for better profitability at the same risk, you should pay attention to what you are reading. MoneyFarm, in fact, is an alternative to deposit accounts because it offers balanced investments with an almost similar degree of risk.

By signing up for MoneyFarm you have the following advantages:
- Personal assistance of a team of competent advisors;
- Choose where to invest by filling in the questionnaire in which you indicate your degree of risk;
- You can start testing the goodness of the platform even with a small capital: just € 500 is enough to try.

With MoneyFarm you can plan your investments and earn up to 5.41% per year, choosing the composition of your portfolio based on your risk profile.

Moneyfarm aims to invest in funds with lower

operating costs and to guarantee maximum transparency to customers.

You can start investing immediately, even with € 500. Before choosing the strategy, the team of experts helps you to plan your goals exactly.

Registration is free: it takes 3 minutes to start to know it, you can also try it on a smartphone as it is really very easy to use.

Unlike many structured platforms for high risk investments (think of trading or options), Moneyfarm allows you to operate even if you have a low risk appetite and is undoubtedly a real alternative to deposit accounts or other banking products that make a lot less.

The portfolios are constantly monitored by a team of experts and free assistance is guaranteed for the entire duration of the relationship.

It is possible to use the live chat service or to set up a telephone appointment thanks to a special toll-free number. The seriousness is certified by the prizes and awards obtained by leading international financial experts and opinions on the web that are definitely positive. You also choose how much you are willing to risk and the staff helps you plan the route step by step.

3. Social Trading

Compared to the previous solution, we are facing a decidedly more risky way: let's underline it immediately, to avoid misunderstandings. If the world of finance interests you, keep reading carefully because you found what you were looking for.

Have you ever tried to approach online trading? If you did and you gave up, most likely you came across the difficulties of a world where only the professional traders, that is, have the experience, years of study and time to constantly monitor what is going on. happening in the market in which they operate.

The social trading we want to talk about is precisely created to solve this gap in skills between professional and non-professional investors. eToro, the first social trading platform, allows you to make copy trading: you can, in other words, copy the winning strategies of top traders emulating their successes.
The principle is simple: by investing as the best, you earn like the best.

Conclusion

Thank for making it through to the end of this book, let's hope it was informative and able to provide you with all of the tools you need to achieve your financial goals.

The next step is to begin to apply what you have learned during the course of this book and get started right away. Our suggestion is always to start by mapping out your investment plan and do the maths many times, before spending real money. Remember that you should never risk more than what you can afford to lose, so manage your capital wisely.

We hope that you find these lessons valuable and that you got the information you were looking for. Letting your money work for you will give you an incredible feeling, especially at the beginning, when you make the first gains. We are thrilled for you to start and we cannot wait to see you buy your first property.